SOULWIND™

BOOK THREE

THE INFAMOUS TRANSIT VAGRANTS

WRITTEN & ILLUSTRATED BY

SCOTT MORSE

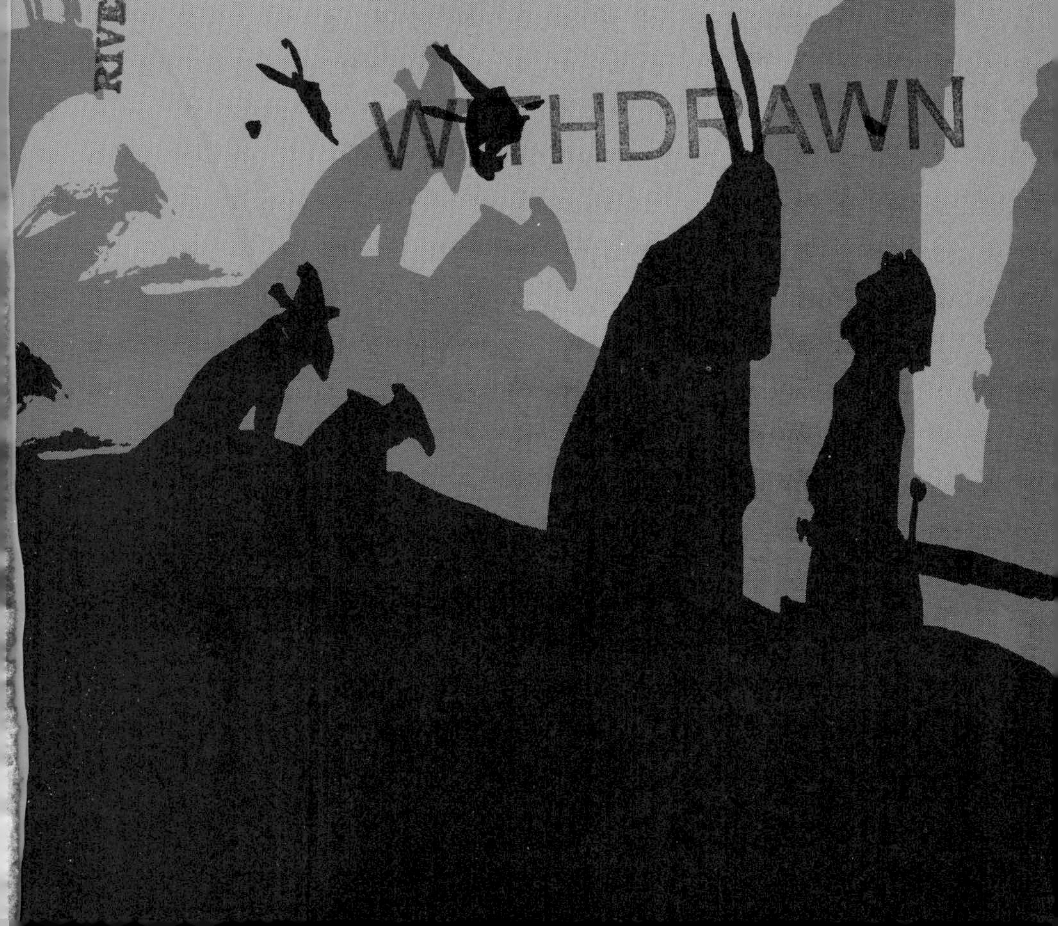

BOOK DESIGN BY
STEVEN BIRCH @ SERVO
EDITED BY
JAMIE S. RICH

PUBLISHED BY ONI PRESS, INC
JOE NOZEMACK
PUBLISHER
JAMIE S. RICH
EDITOR IN CHIEF
JAMES LUCAS JONES
ASSITANT EDITOR / WEBMASTER

ONI PRESS, INC.
6336 SE Milwaukie Avenue, Suite 30
Portland, OR 97202
USA

www.onipress.com

First edition: August 2000
ISBN 0-9667127-7-3

1 3 5 7 9 10 8 6 4 2
PRINTED IN CANADA.

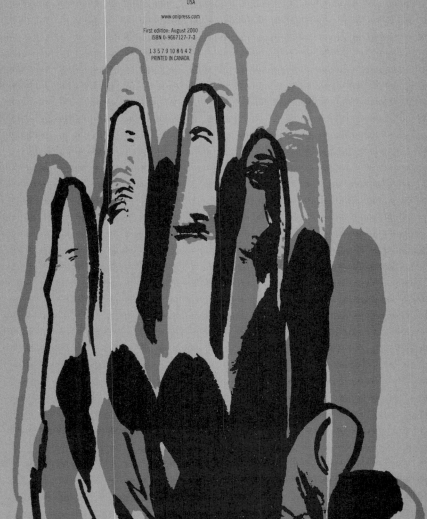

THE BOY, ONE
AFTERNOON, WENT
FOR A WALK WITH
ONE OF THE ELDERS.

THE BOY DIDN'T
SAY A THING, BUT
HIS SIFU TALKED
QUITE A BIT.

HE SAID, "COME ON.
SIFU'S TALKING.

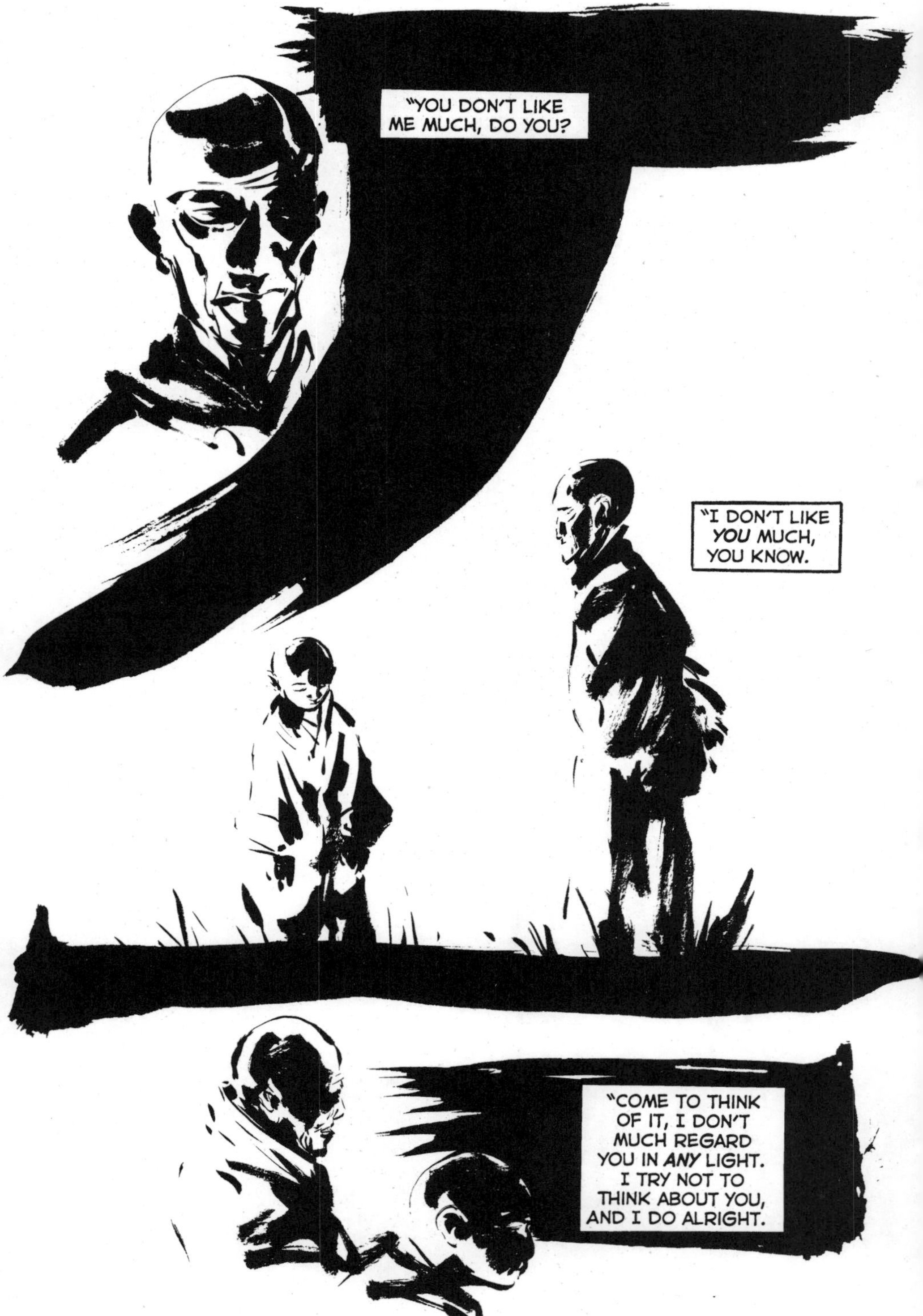
"YOU DON'T LIKE ME MUCH, DO YOU?
"I DON'T LIKE *YOU* MUCH, YOU KNOW.
"COME TO THINK OF IT, I DON'T MUCH REGARD YOU IN *ANY* LIGHT. I TRY NOT TO THINK ABOUT YOU, AND I DO ALRIGHT.

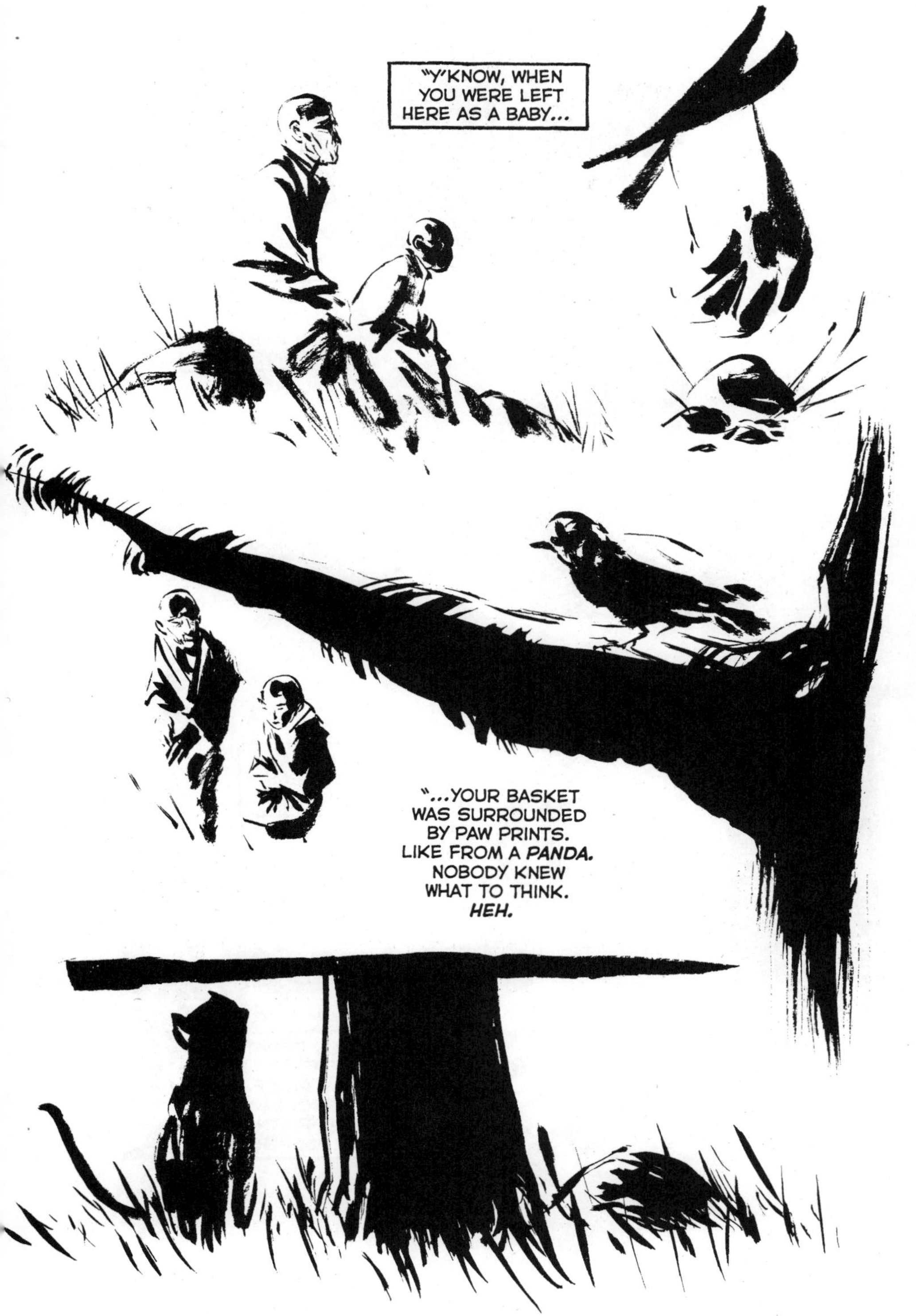
"Y'KNOW, WHEN YOU WERE LEFT HERE AS A BABY...
"...YOUR BASKET WAS SURROUNDED BY PAW PRINTS. LIKE FROM A PANDA. NOBODY KNEW WHAT TO THINK. HEH.

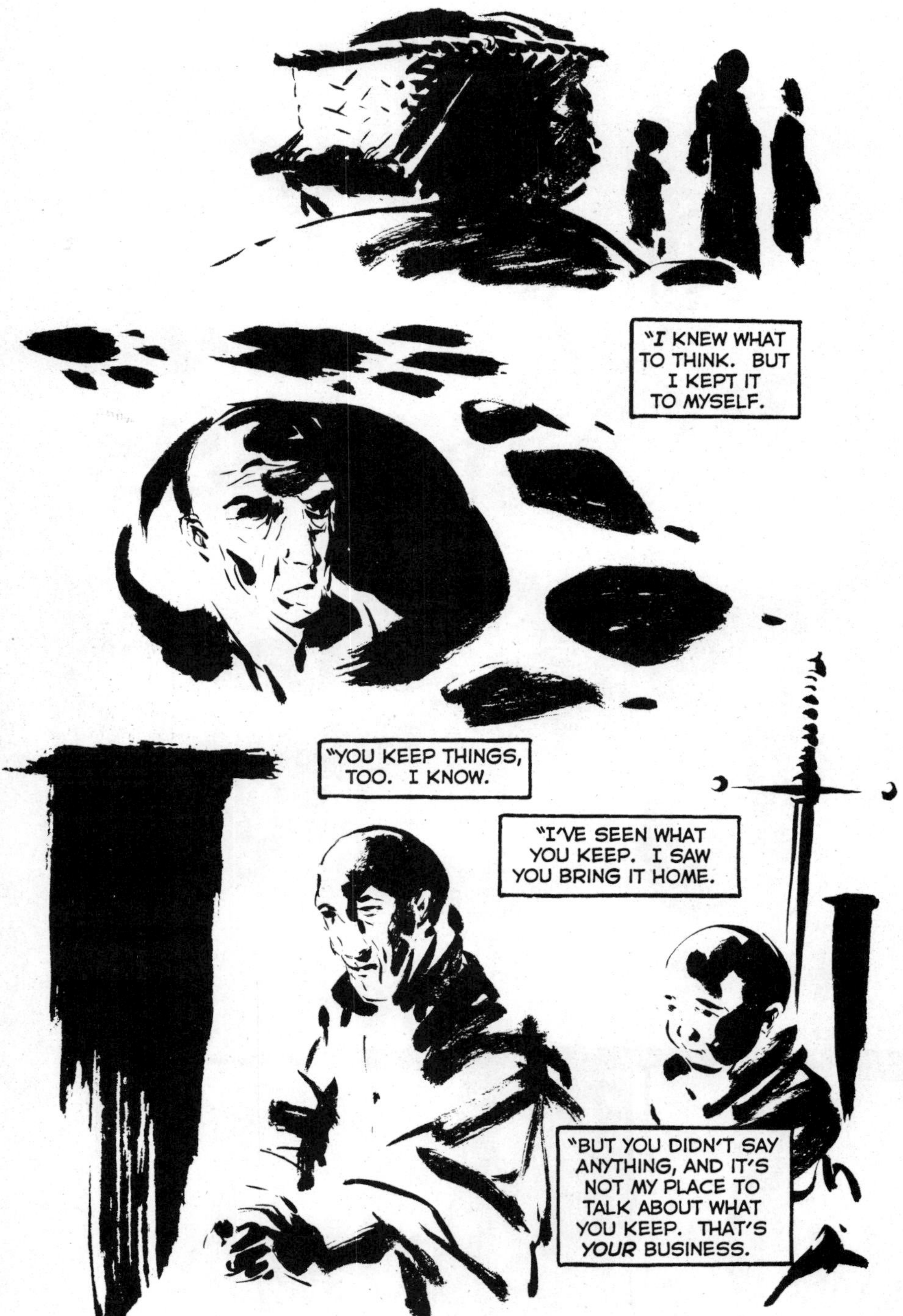
"I KNEW WHAT TO THINK. BUT I KEPT IT TO MYSELF.
"YOU KEEP THINGS, TOO. I KNOW.
"I'VE SEEN WHAT YOU KEEP. I SAW YOU BRING IT HOME.
"BUT YOU DIDN'T SAY ANYTHING, AND IT'S NOT MY PLACE TO TALK ABOUT WHAT YOU KEEP. THAT'S *YOUR* BUSINESS.

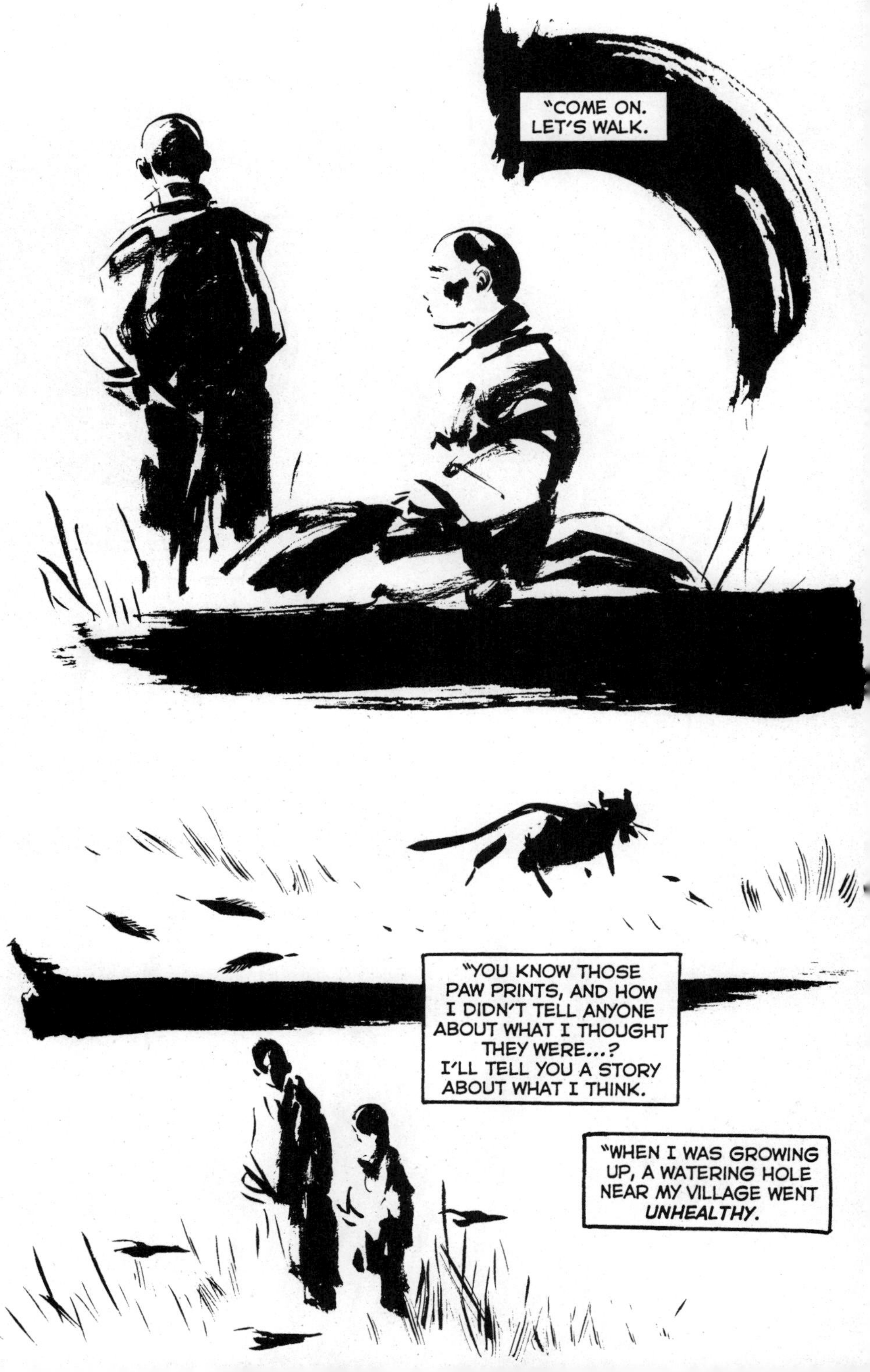
"COME ON. LET'S WALK.
"YOU KNOW THOSE PAW PRINTS, AND HOW I DIDN'T TELL ANYONE ABOUT WHAT I THOUGHT THEY WERE...? I'LL TELL YOU A STORY ABOUT WHAT I THINK.
"WHEN I WAS GROWING UP, A WATERING HOLE NEAR MY VILLAGE WENT *UNHEALTHY*.

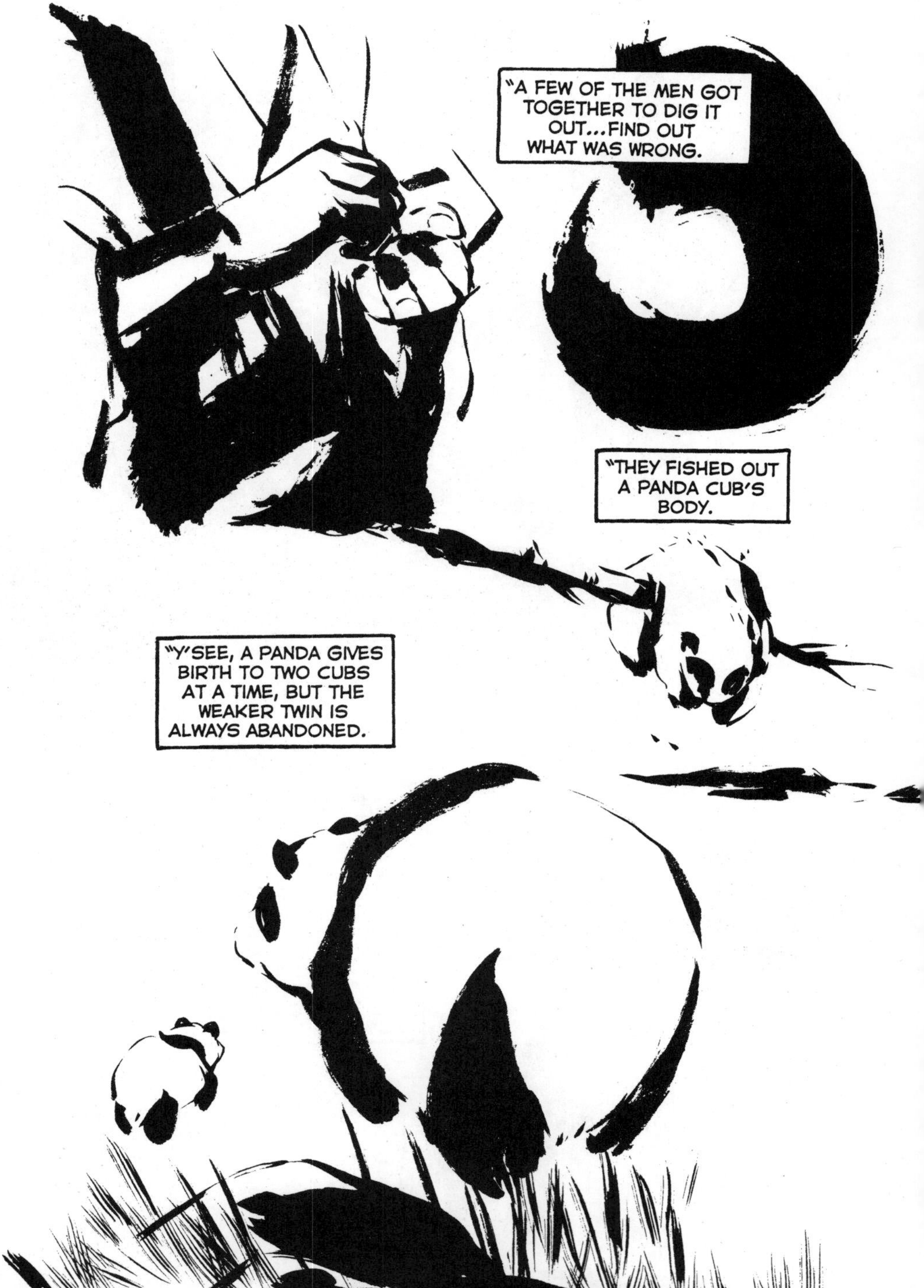
"A FEW OF THE MEN GOT TOGETHER TO DIG IT OUT...FIND OUT WHAT WAS WRONG.
"THEY FISHED OUT A PANDA CUB'S BODY.
"Y'SEE, A PANDA GIVES BIRTH TO TWO CUBS AT A TIME, BUT THE WEAKER TWIN IS ALWAYS ABANDONED.

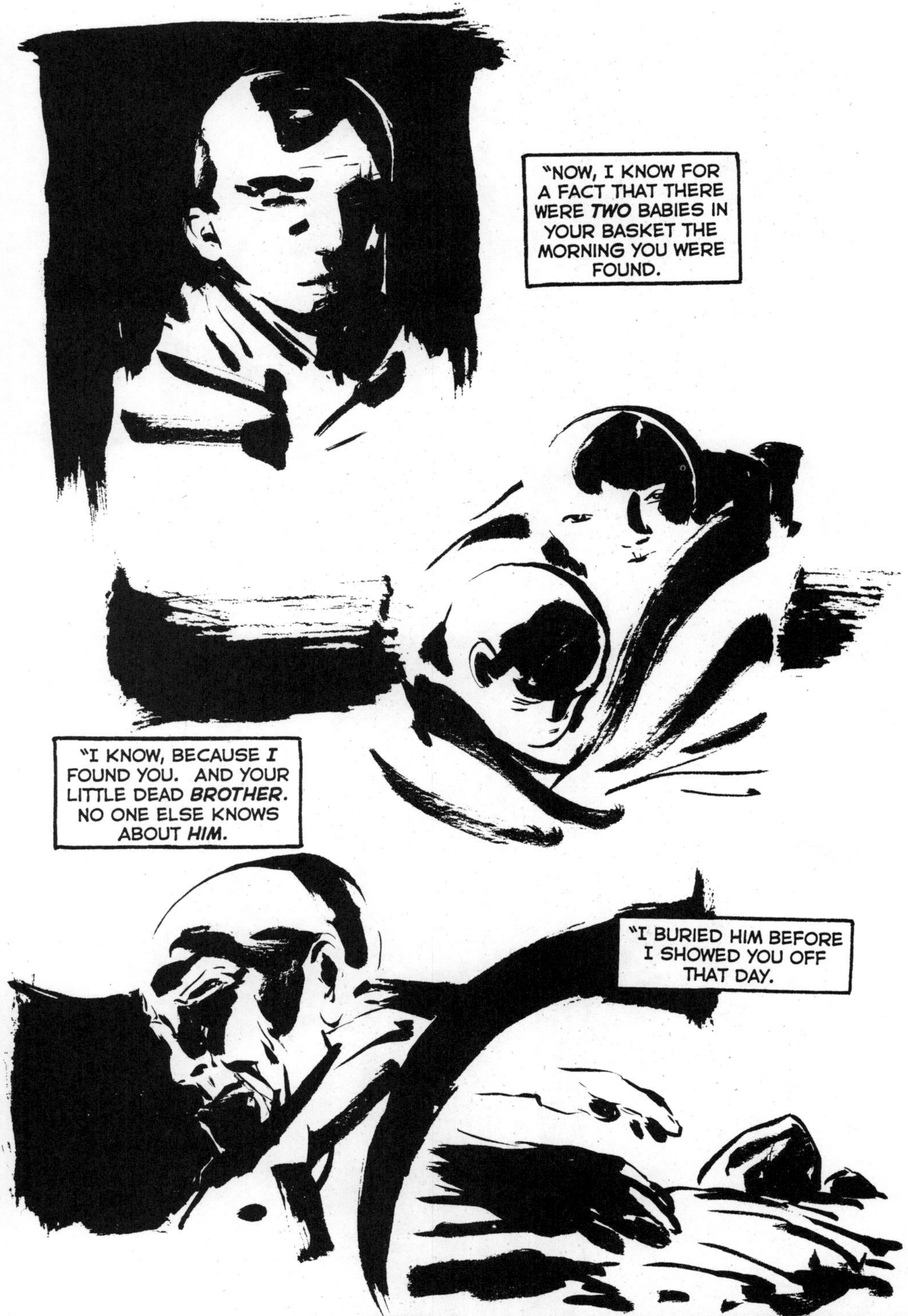
"NOW, I KNOW FOR A FACT THAT THERE WERE *TWO* BABIES IN YOUR BASKET THE MORNING YOU WERE FOUND.
"I KNOW, BECAUSE *I* FOUND YOU. AND YOUR LITTLE DEAD *BROTHER*. NO ONE ELSE KNOWS ABOUT *HIM*.
"I BURIED HIM BEFORE I SHOWED YOU OFF THAT DAY.

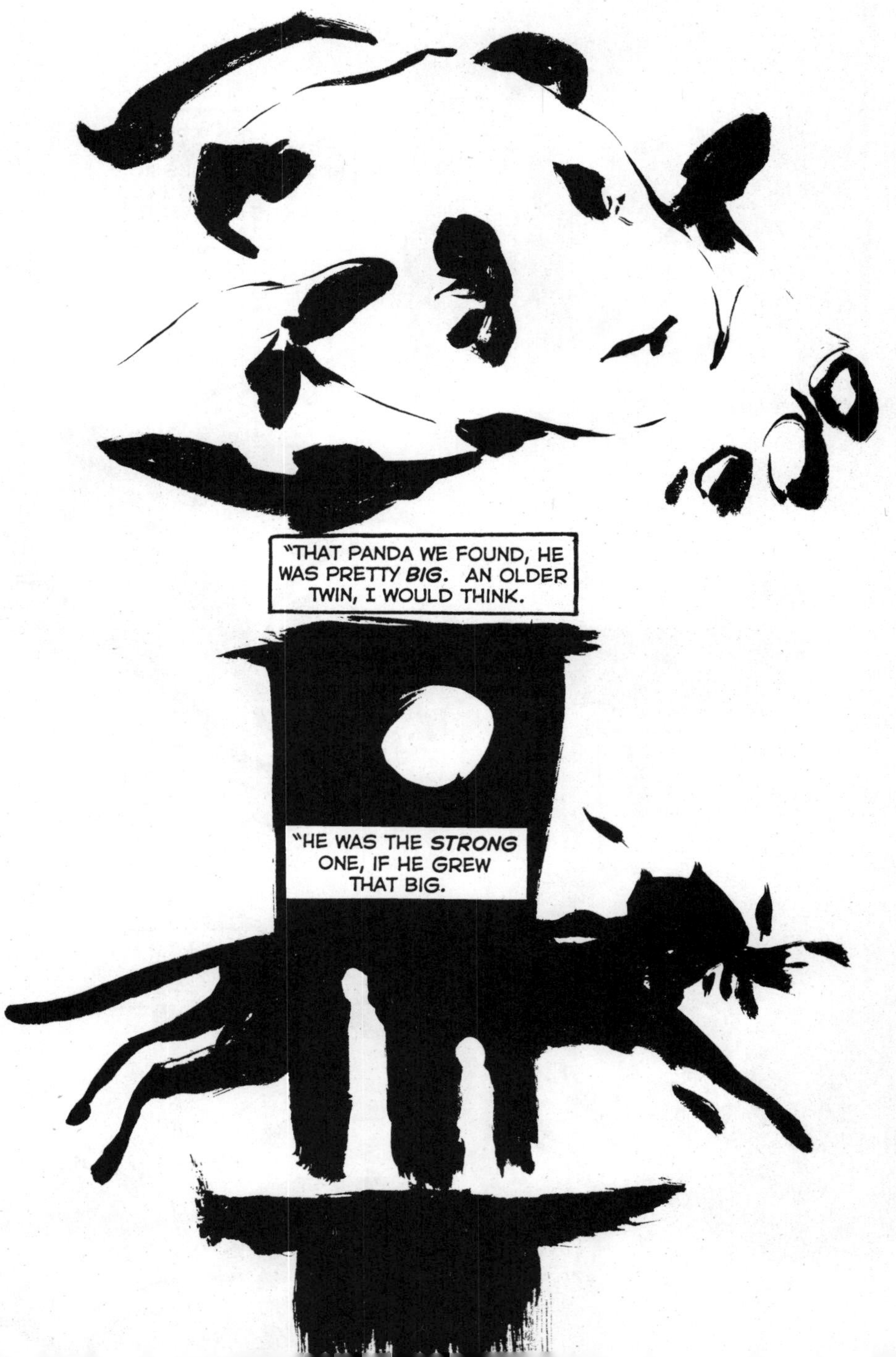
"THAT PANDA WE FOUND, HE WAS PRETTY *BIG*. AN OLDER TWIN, I WOULD THINK.
"HE WAS THE *STRONG* ONE, IF HE GREW THAT BIG.

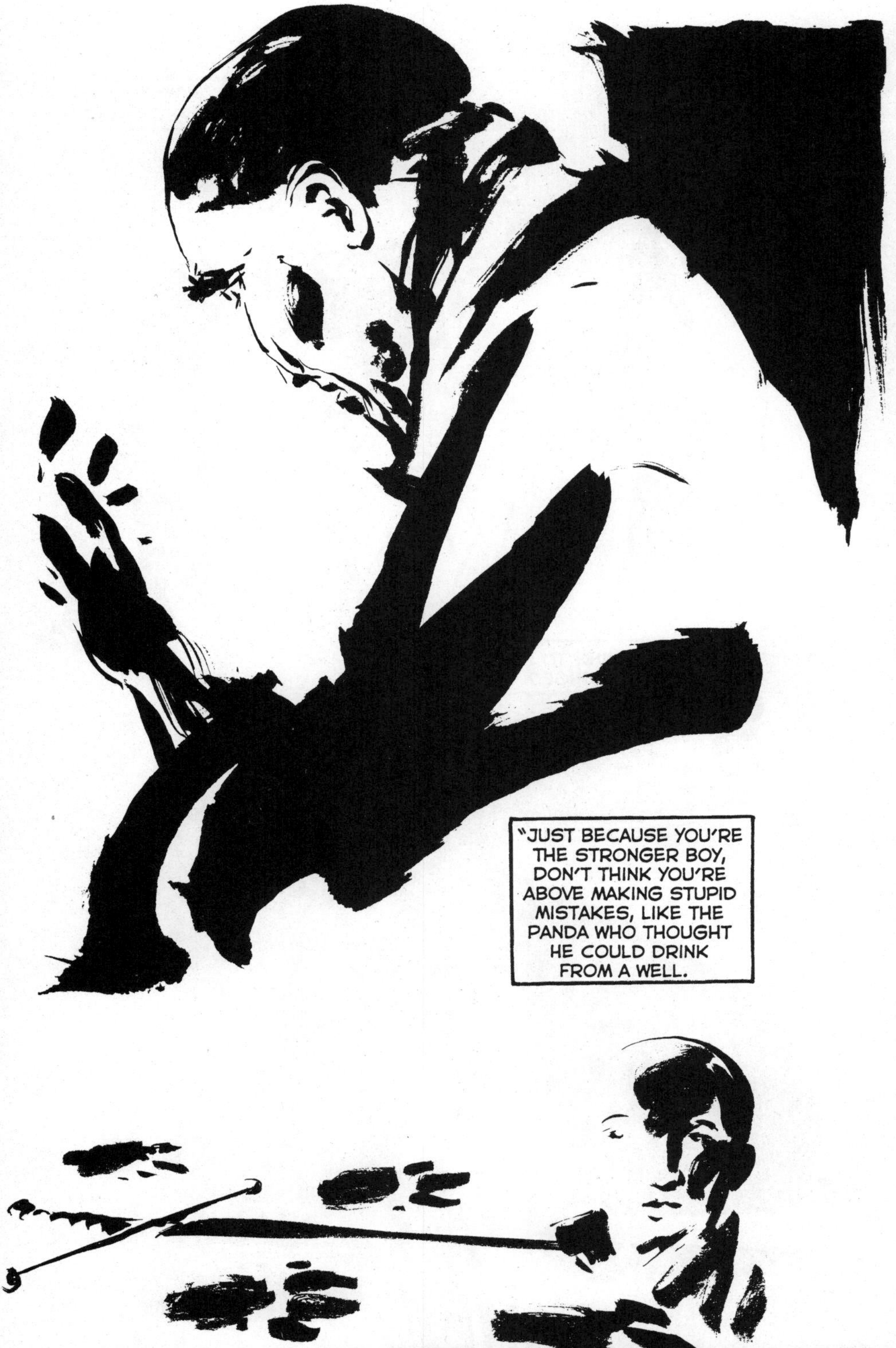
"JUST BECAUSE YOU'RE THE STRONGER BOY, DON'T THINK YOU'RE ABOVE MAKING STUPID MISTAKES, LIKE THE PANDA WHO THOUGHT HE COULD DRINK FROM A WELL.

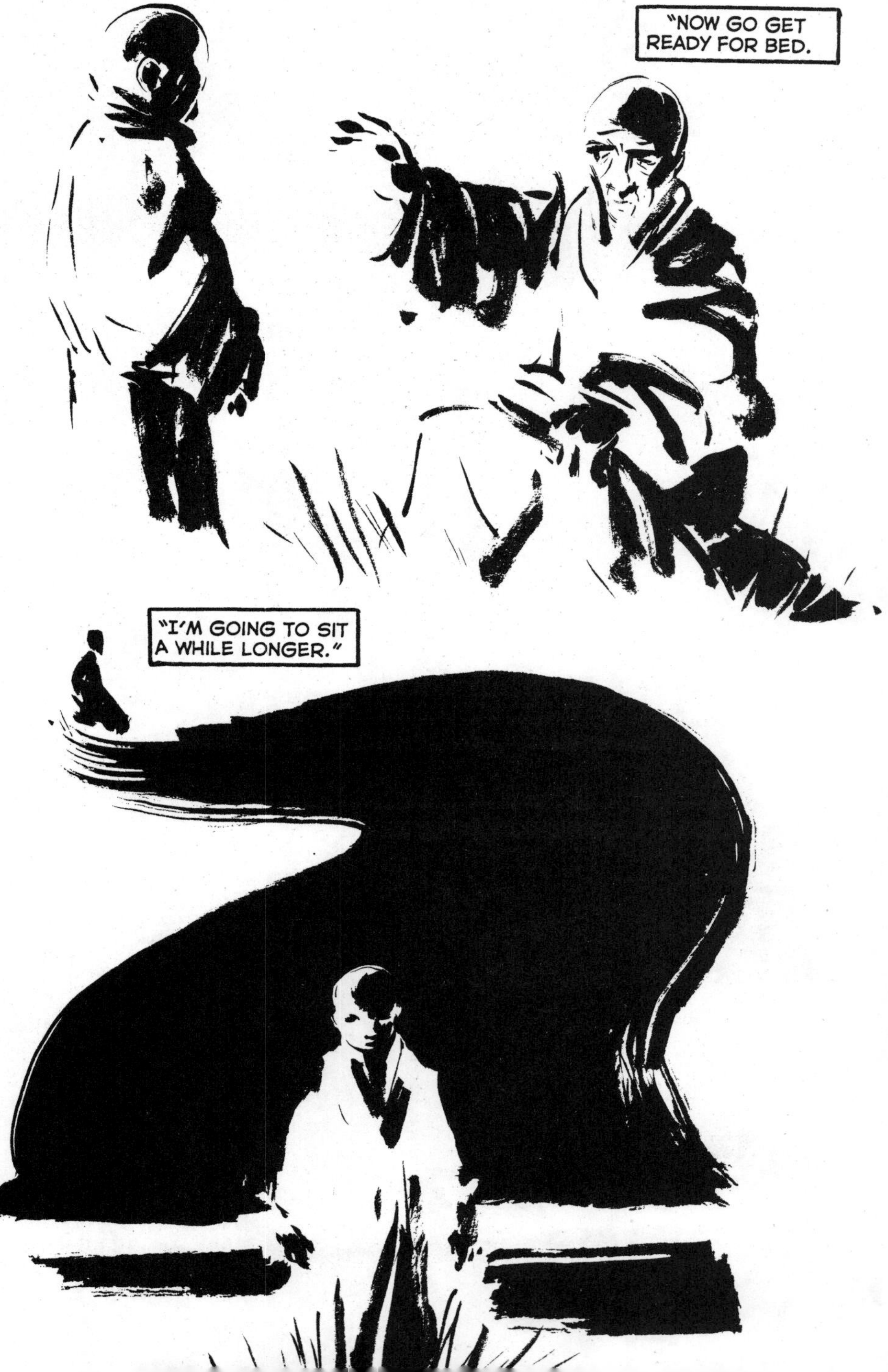
"NOW GO GET
READY FOR BED.
"I'M GOING TO SIT
A WHILE LONGER."

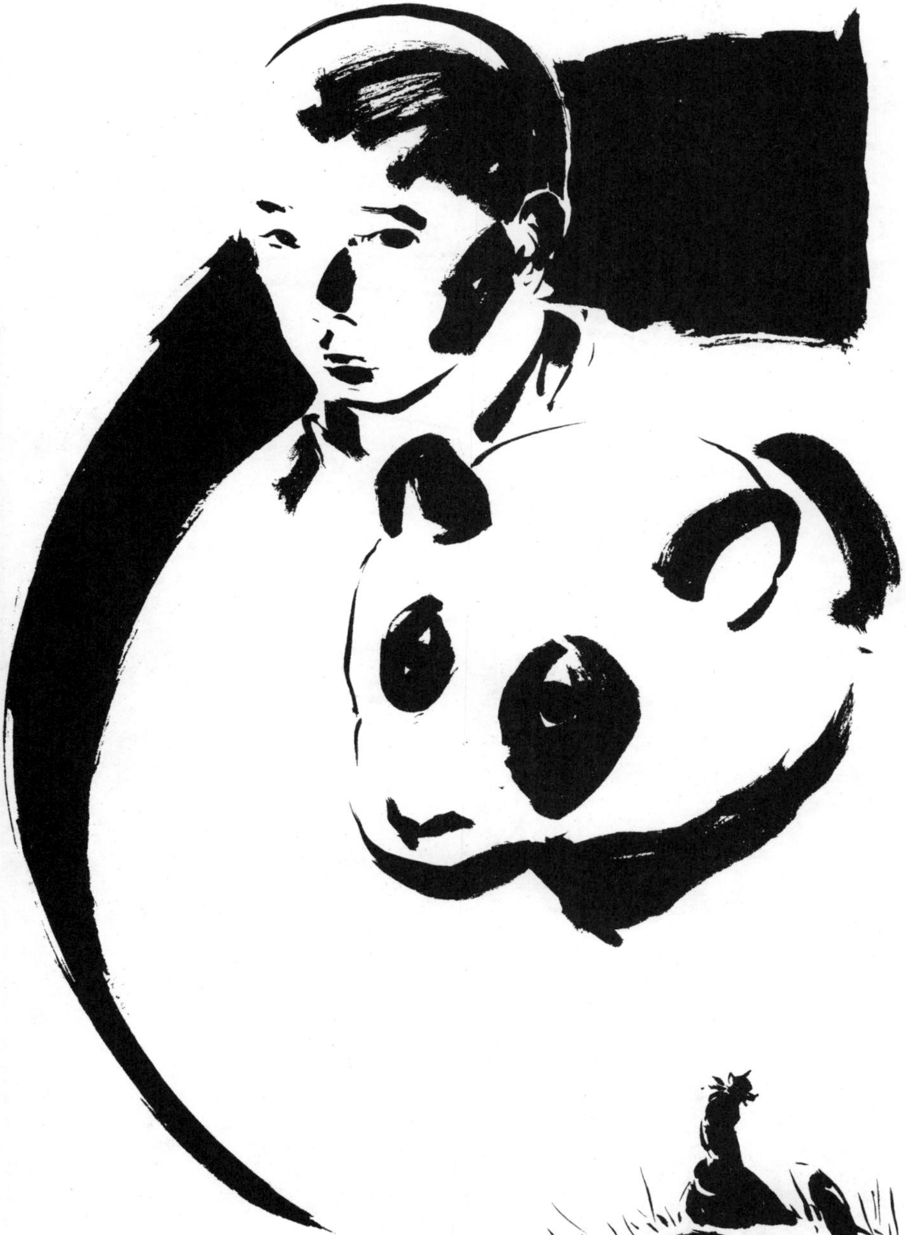

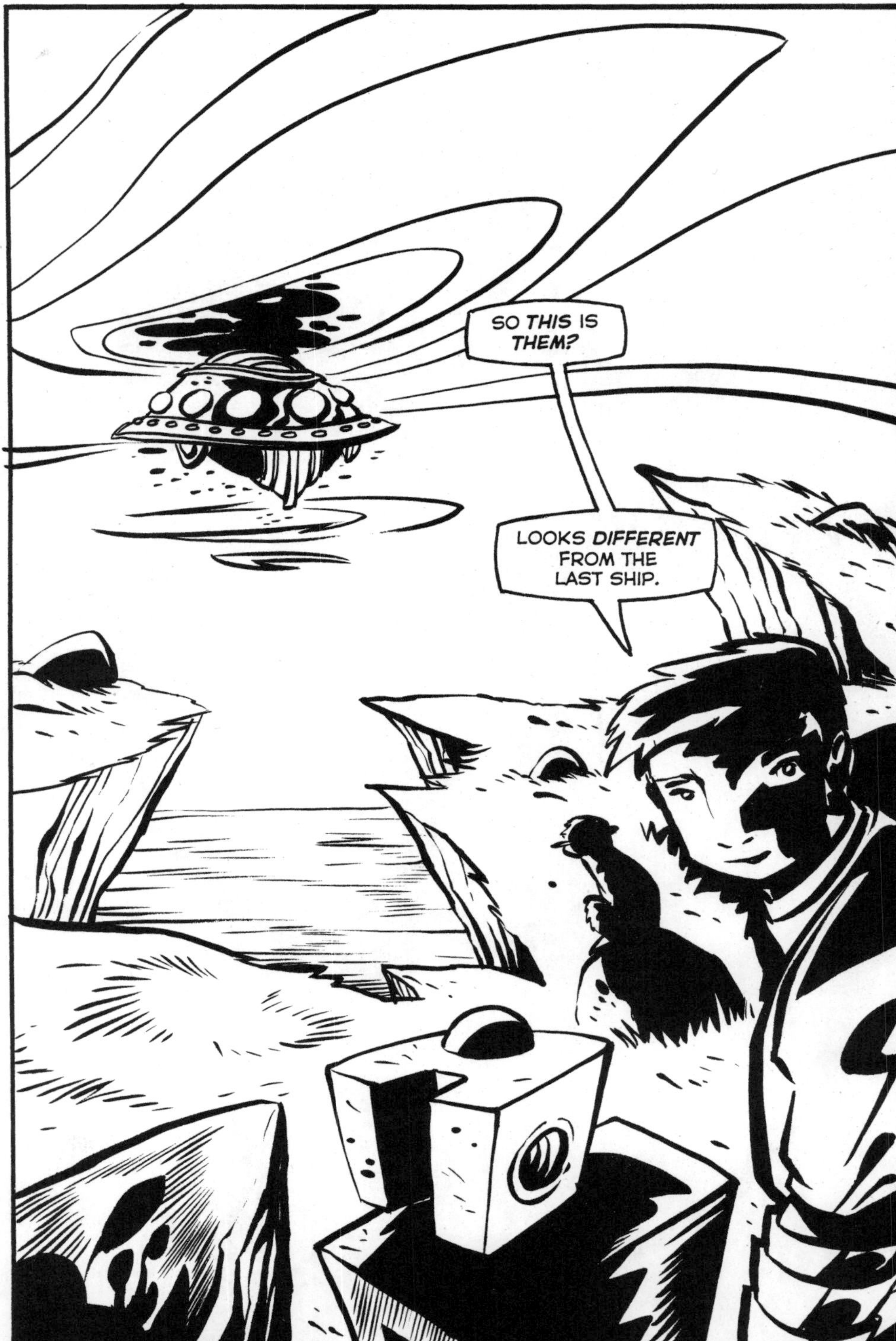
SO *THIS* IS *THEM?*
LOOKS *DIFFERENT* FROM THE LAST SHIP.

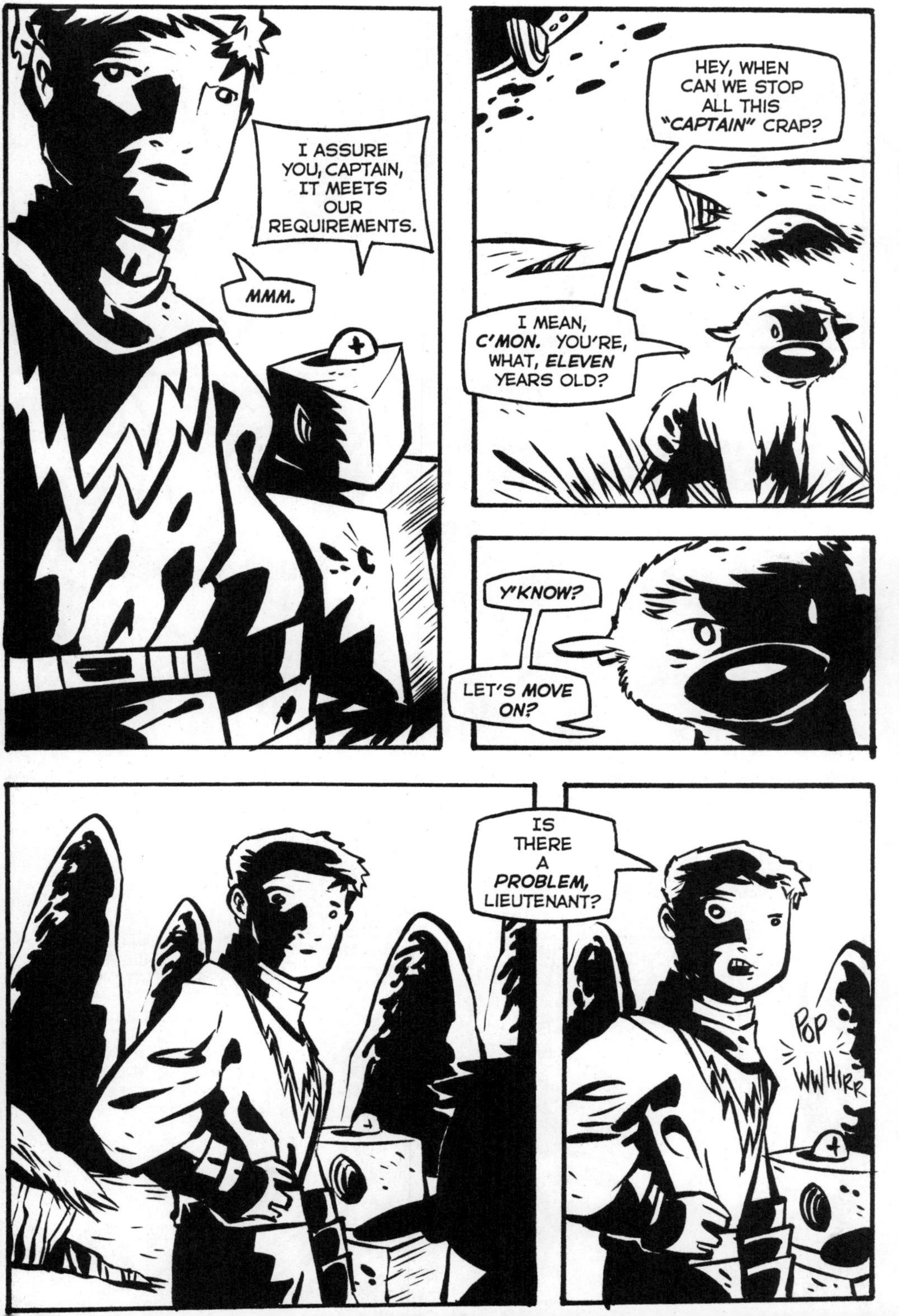
I ASSURE YOU, CAPTAIN, IT MEETS OUR REQUIREMENTS.
MMM.
HEY, WHEN CAN WE STOP ALL THIS "CAPTAIN" CRAP?
I MEAN, C'MON. YOU'RE, WHAT, ELEVEN YEARS OLD?
Y'KNOW?
LET'S MOVE ON?
IS THERE A PROBLEM, LIEUTENANT?
POP
WWHIRR

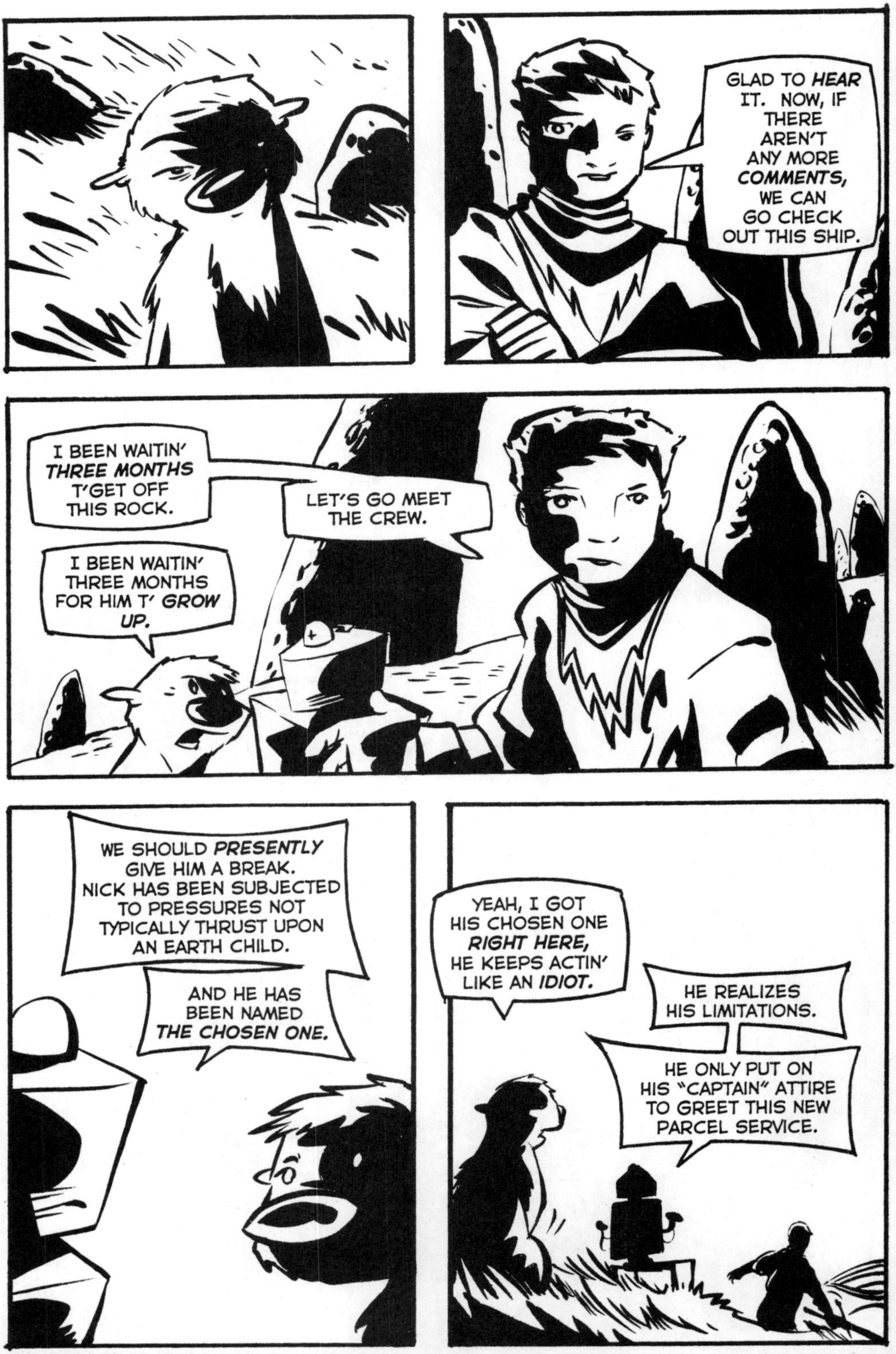
GLAD TO *HEAR* IT. NOW, IF THERE AREN'T ANY MORE *COMMENTS,* WE CAN GO CHECK OUT THIS SHIP.
I BEEN WAITIN' *THREE MONTHS* T'GET OFF THIS ROCK.
LET'S GO MEET THE CREW.
I BEEN WAITIN' THREE MONTHS FOR HIM T' *GROW UP.*
WE SHOULD *PRESENTLY* GIVE HIM A BREAK. NICK HAS BEEN SUBJECTED TO PRESSURES NOT TYPICALLY THRUST UPON AN EARTH CHILD.
AND HE HAS BEEN NAMED *THE CHOSEN ONE.*
YEAH, I GOT HIS CHOSEN ONE *RIGHT HERE,* HE KEEPS ACTIN' LIKE AN *IDIOT.*
HE REALIZES HIS LIMITATIONS.
HE ONLY PUT ON HIS "CAPTAIN" ATTIRE TO GREET THIS NEW PARCEL SERVICE.

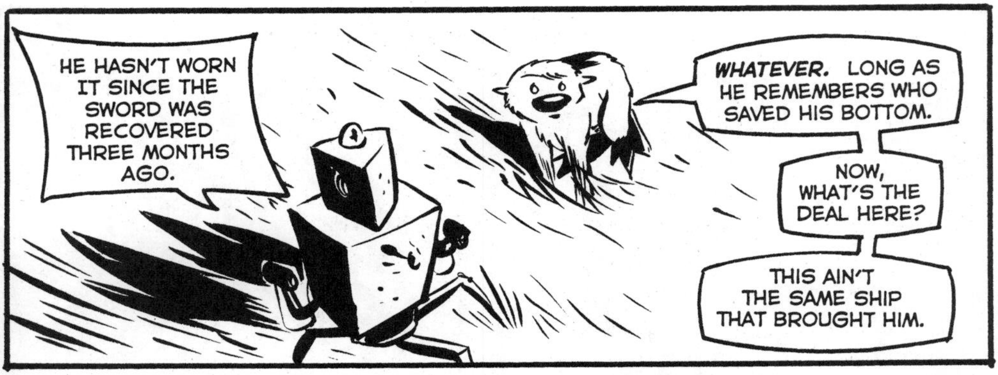
HE HASN'T WORN IT SINCE THE SWORD WAS RECOVERED THREE MONTHS AGO.
WHATEVER. LONG AS HE REMEMBERS WHO SAVED HIS BOTTOM.
NOW, WHAT'S THE DEAL HERE?
THIS AIN'T THE SAME SHIP THAT BROUGHT HIM.

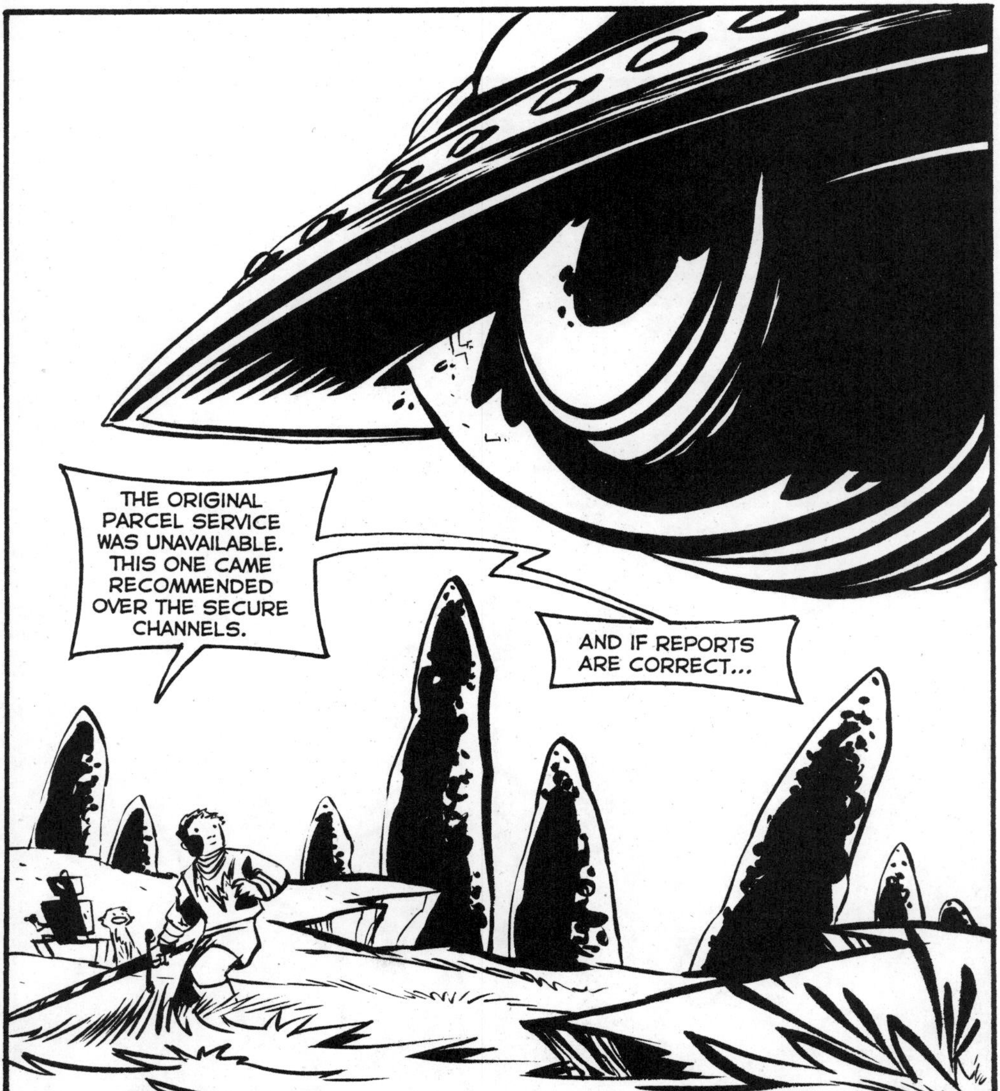
THE ORIGINAL PARCEL SERVICE WAS UNAVAILABLE. THIS ONE CAME RECOMMENDED OVER THE SECURE CHANNELS.
AND IF REPORTS ARE CORRECT...

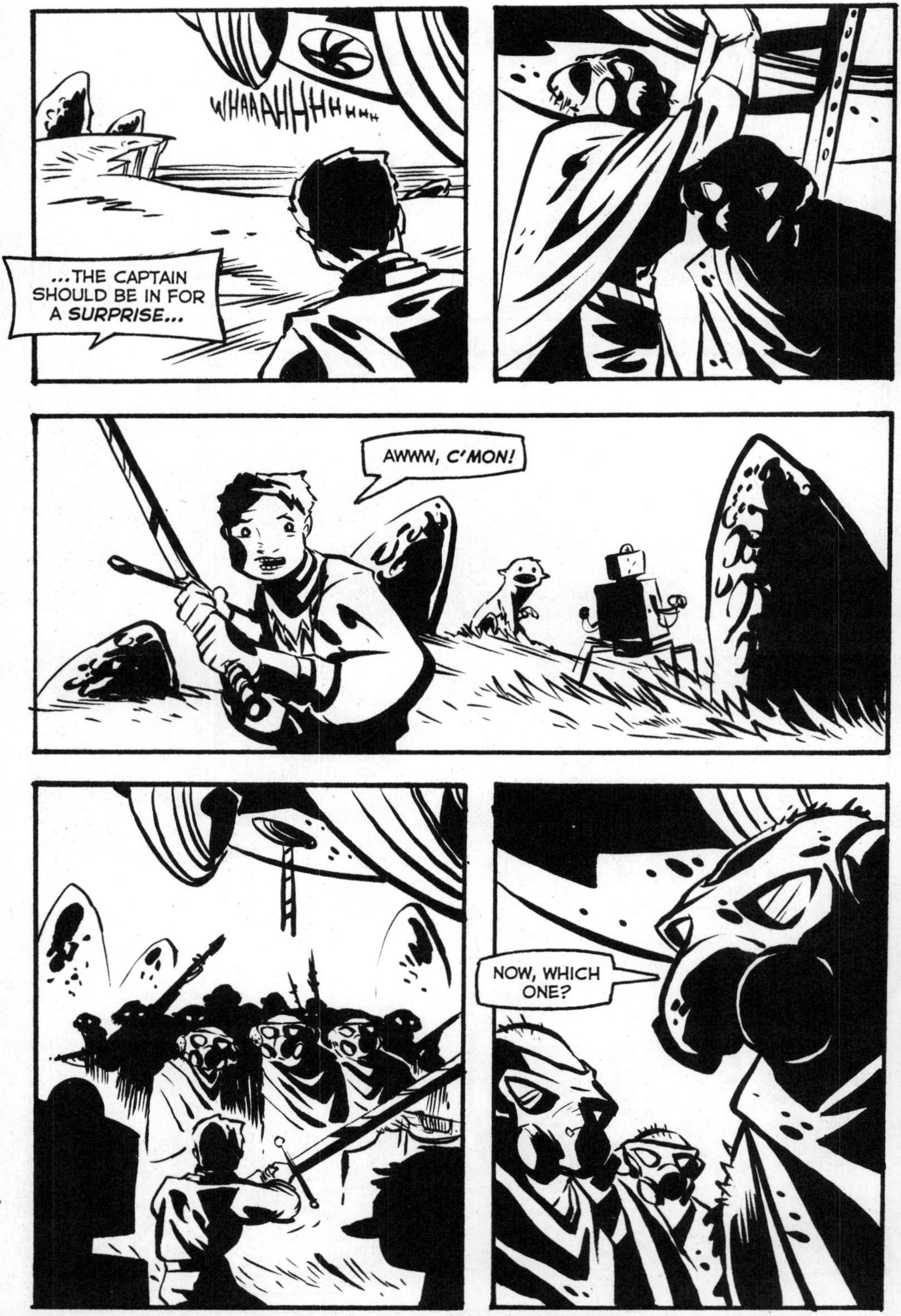
WHAAAHHHHHHHH
...THE CAPTAIN SHOULD BE IN FOR A SURPRISE...
AWWW, C'MON!
NOW, WHICH ONE?

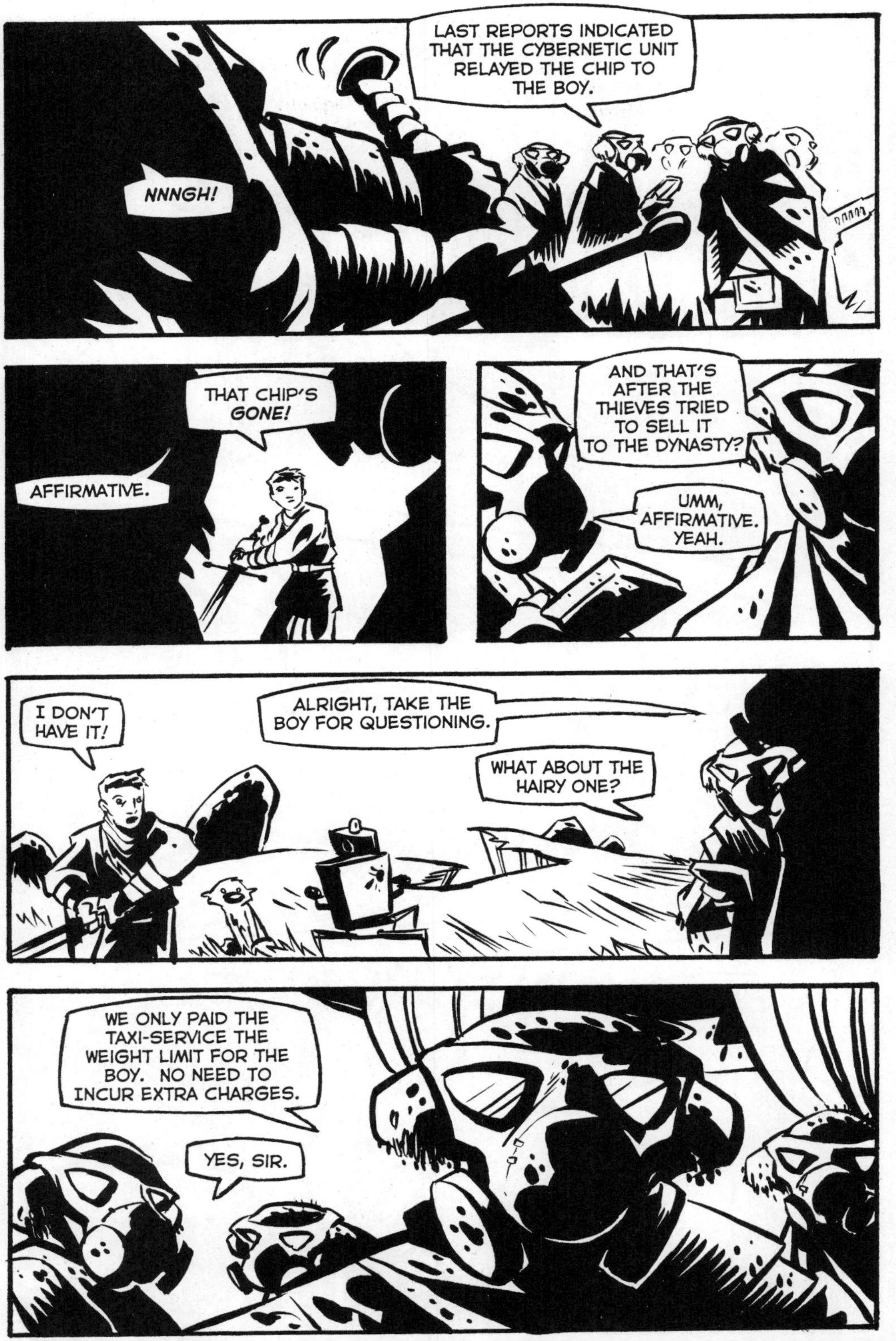
LAST REPORTS INDICATED THAT THE CYBERNETIC UNIT RELAYED THE CHIP TO THE BOY.
NNNGH!
THAT CHIP'S GONE!
AFFIRMATIVE.
AND THAT'S AFTER THE THIEVES TRIED TO SELL IT TO THE DYNASTY?
UMM, AFFIRMATIVE. YEAH.
I DON'T HAVE IT!
ALRIGHT, TAKE THE BOY FOR QUESTIONING.
WHAT ABOUT THE HAIRY ONE?
WE ONLY PAID THE TAXI-SERVICE THE WEIGHT LIMIT FOR THE BOY. NO NEED TO INCUR EXTRA CHARGES.
YES, SIR.

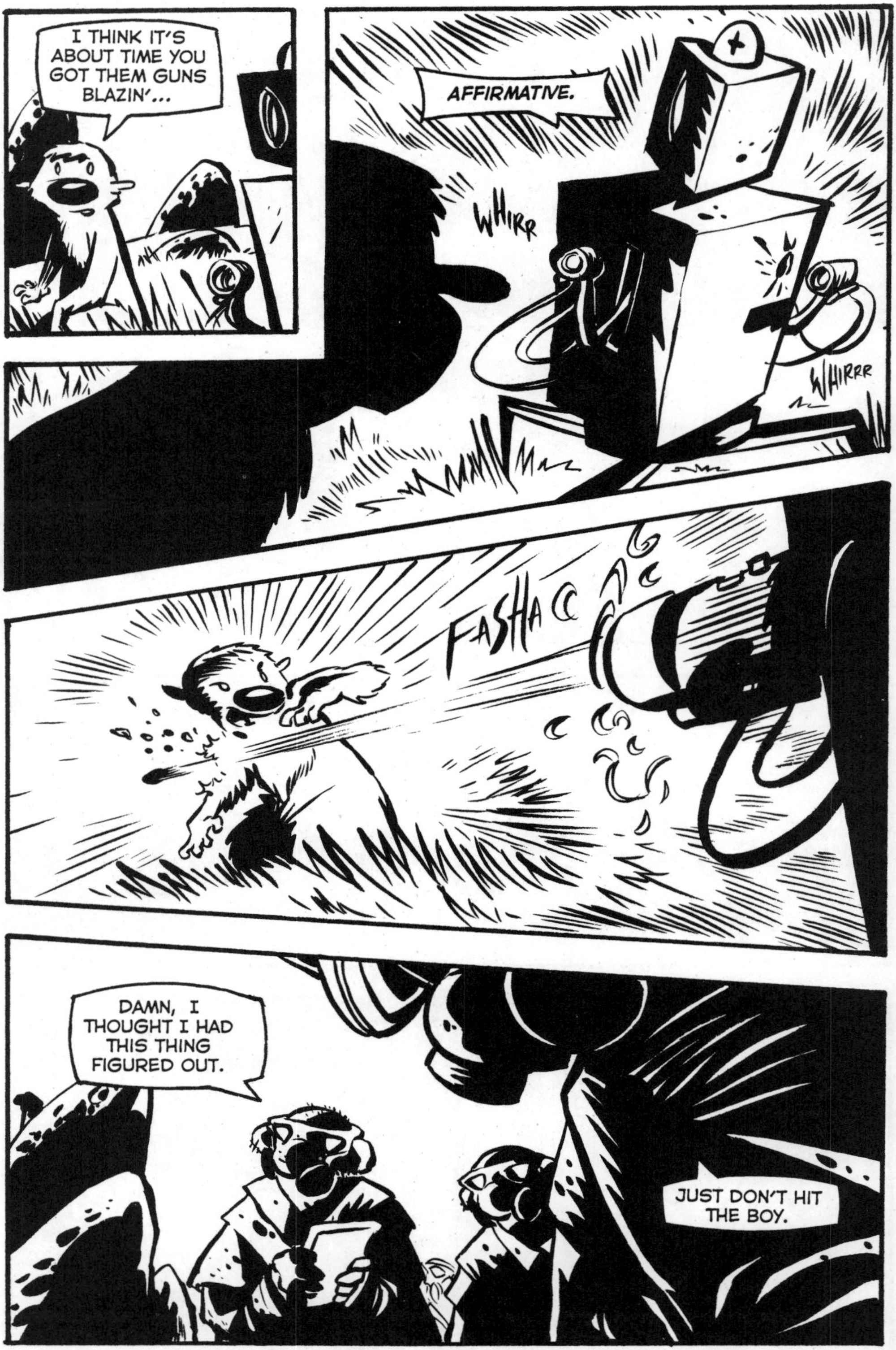
I THINK IT'S ABOUT TIME YOU GOT THEM GUNS BLAZIN'...
AFFIRMATIVE.
WHIRR
WHIRRR
FASHA
DAMN, I THOUGHT I HAD THIS THING FIGURED OUT.
JUST DON'T HIT THE BOY.

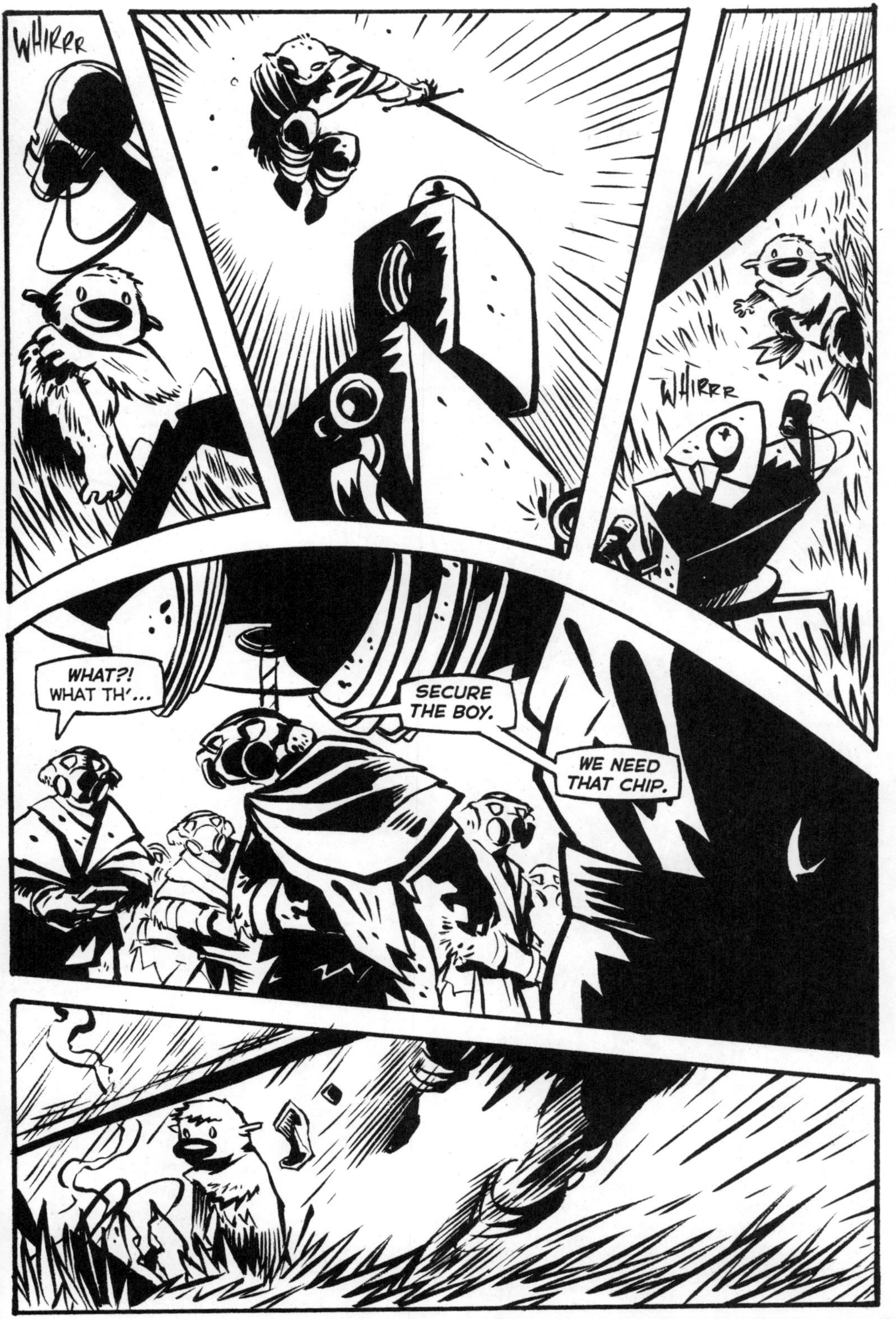
WHIRRR
WHIRRR
WHAT?! WHAT TH'...
SECURE THE BOY.
WE NEED THAT CHIP.

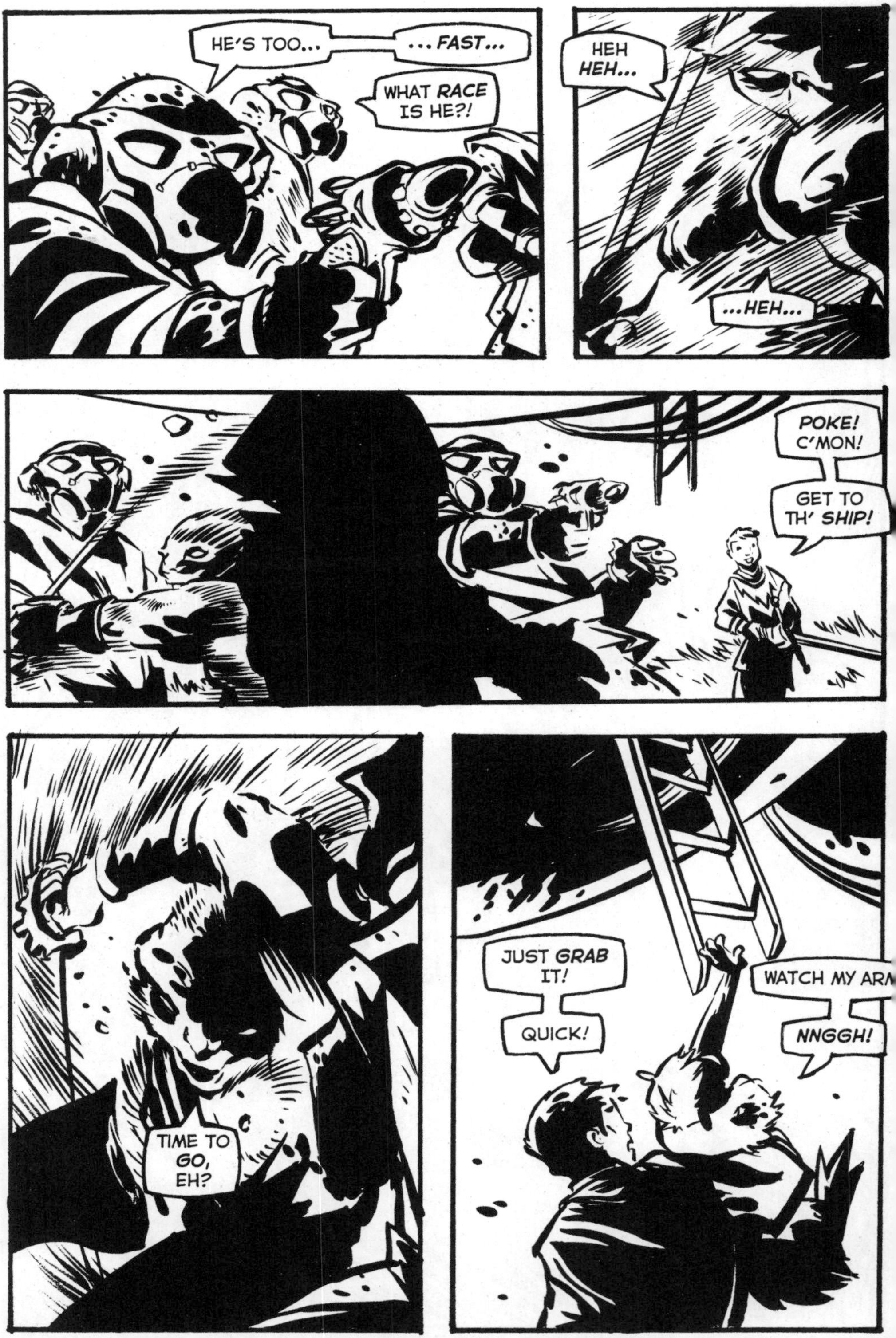
HE'S TOO...
...FAST...
WHAT RACE IS HE?!
HEH HEH...
...HEH...
POKE! C'MON!
GET TO TH' SHIP!
TIME TO GO, EH?
JUST GRAB IT!
QUICK!
WATCH MY AR
NNGGH!

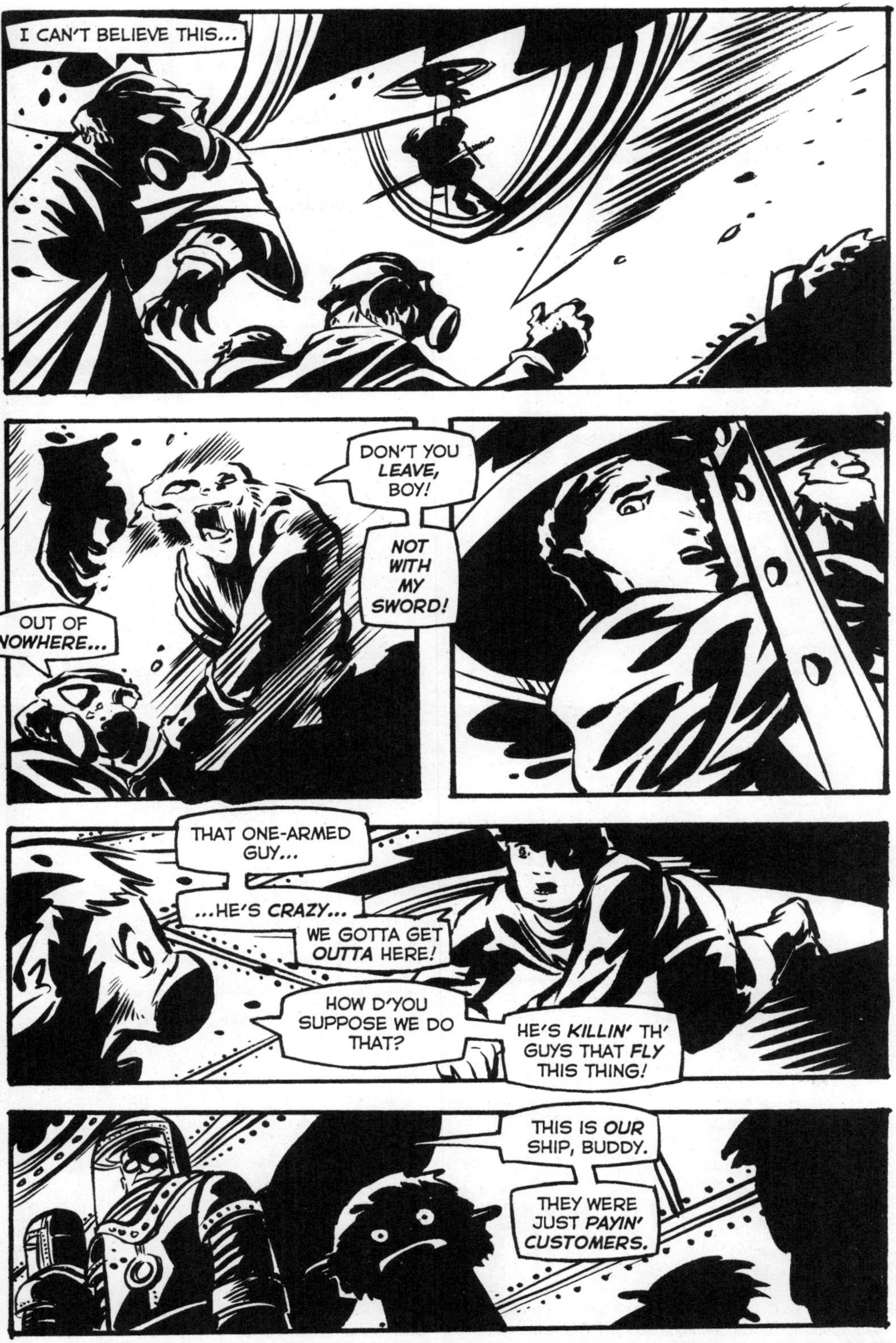
I CAN'T BELIEVE THIS...
OUT OF NOWHERE...
DON'T YOU LEAVE, BOY!
NOT WITH MY SWORD!
THAT ONE-ARMED GUY...
...HE'S CRAZY...
WE GOTTA GET OUTTA HERE!
HOW D'YOU SUPPOSE WE DO THAT?
HE'S KILLIN' TH' GUYS THAT FLY THIS THING!
THIS IS OUR SHIP, BUDDY.
THEY WERE JUST PAYIN' CUSTOMERS.

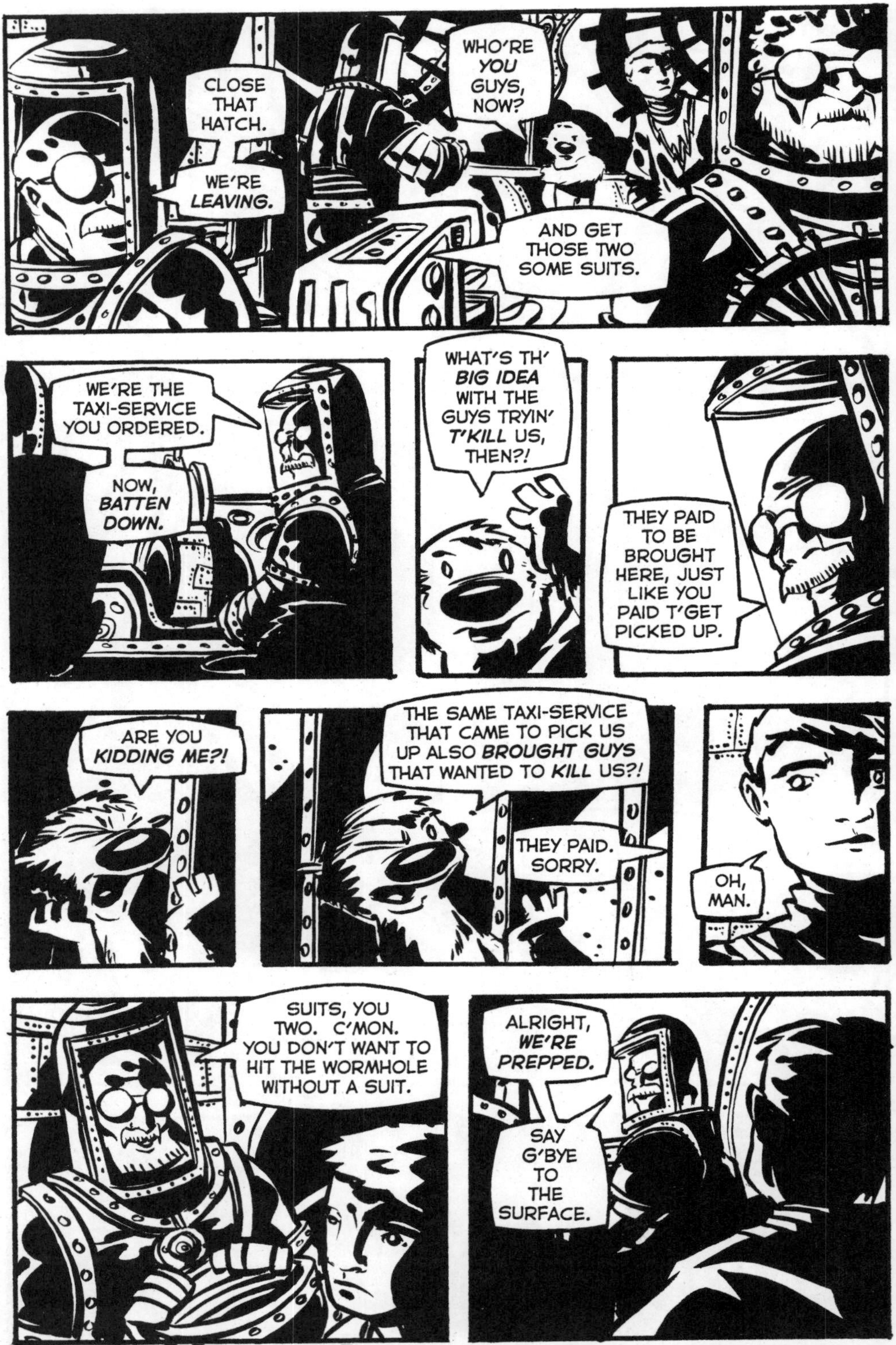
CLOSE THAT HATCH.
WE'RE *LEAVING.*
WHO'RE *YOU* GUYS, NOW?
AND GET THOSE TWO SOME SUITS.
WE'RE THE TAXI-SERVICE YOU ORDERED.
NOW, *BATTEN DOWN.*
WHAT'S TH' *BIG IDEA* WITH THE GUYS TRYIN' *T'KILL* US, THEN?!
THEY PAID TO BE BROUGHT HERE, JUST LIKE YOU PAID T'GET PICKED UP.
ARE YOU *KIDDING ME?!*
THE SAME TAXI-SERVICE THAT CAME TO PICK US UP ALSO *BROUGHT GUYS* THAT WANTED TO *KILL* US?!
THEY PAID. SORRY.
OH, MAN.
SUITS, YOU TWO. C'MON. YOU DON'T WANT TO HIT THE WORMHOLE WITHOUT A SUIT.
ALRIGHT, *WE'RE PREPPED.*
SAY G'BYE TO THE SURFACE.

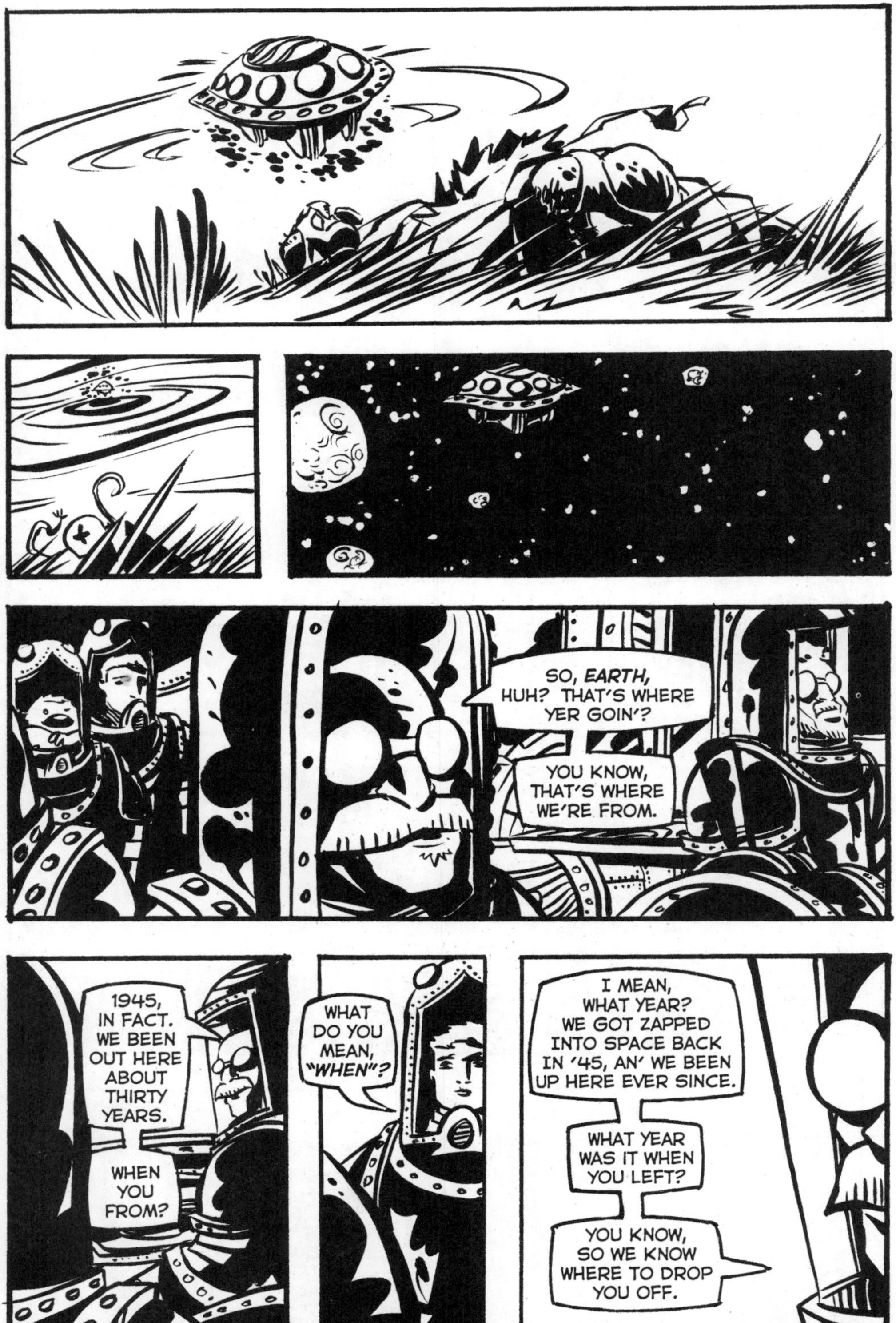

SO, *EARTH,* HUH? THAT'S WHERE YER GOIN'?
YOU KNOW, THAT'S WHERE WE'RE FROM.
1945, IN FACT. WE BEEN OUT HERE ABOUT THIRTY YEARS.
WHEN YOU FROM?
WHAT DO YOU MEAN, *"WHEN"*?
I MEAN, WHAT YEAR? WE GOT ZAPPED INTO SPACE BACK IN '45, AN' WE BEEN UP HERE EVER SINCE.
WHAT YEAR WAS IT WHEN YOU LEFT?
YOU KNOW, SO WE KNOW WHERE TO DROP YOU OFF.

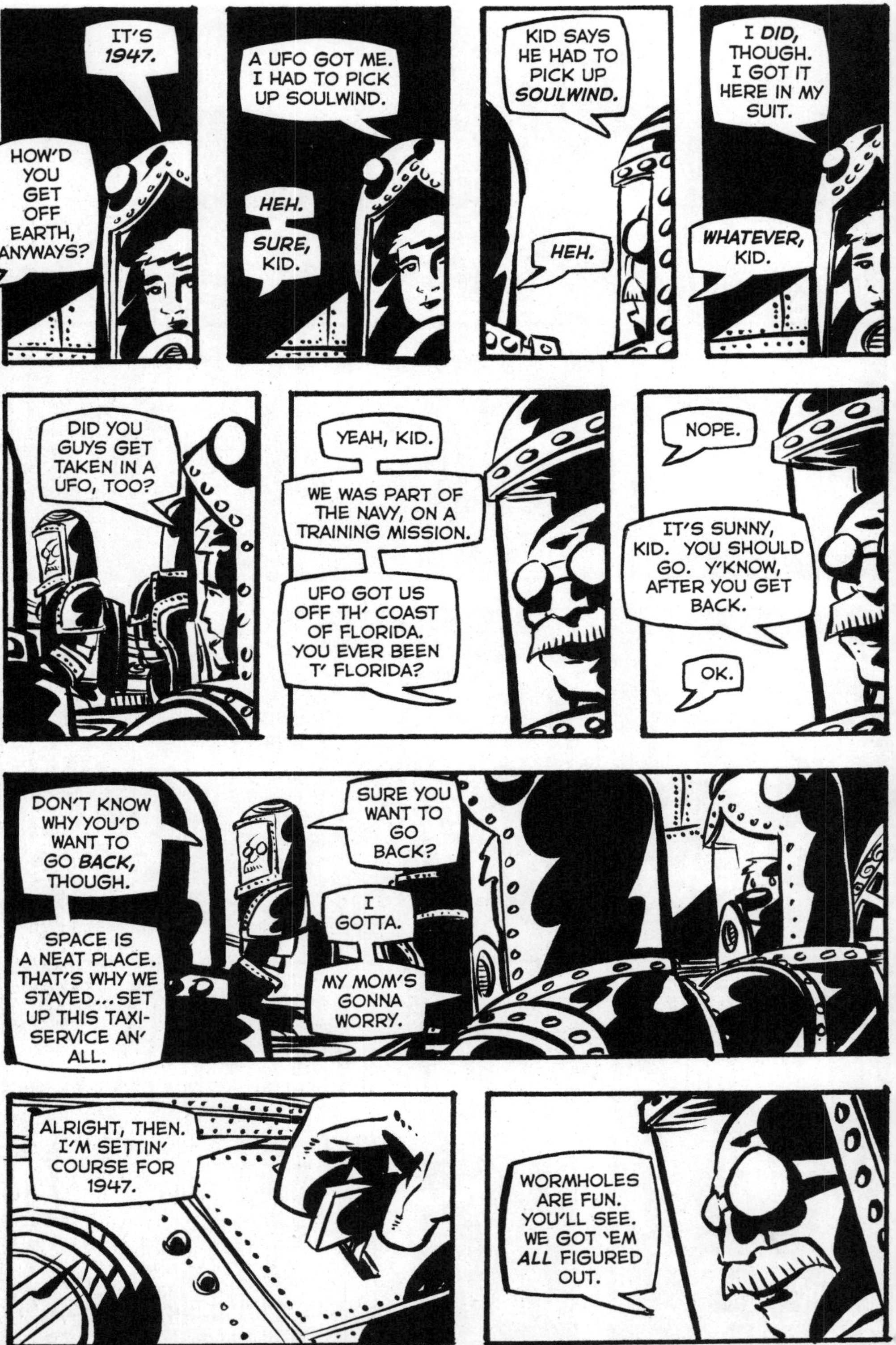
IT'S *1947.*
HOW'D YOU GET OFF EARTH, ANYWAYS?
A UFO GOT ME. I HAD TO PICK UP SOULWIND.
HEH.
SURE, KID.
KID SAYS HE HAD TO PICK UP *SOULWIND.*
HEH.
I *DID,* THOUGH. I GOT IT HERE IN MY SUIT.
WHATEVER, KID.
DID YOU GUYS GET TAKEN IN A UFO, TOO?
YEAH, KID.
WE WAS PART OF THE NAVY, ON A TRAINING MISSION.
UFO GOT US OFF TH' COAST OF FLORIDA. YOU EVER BEEN T' FLORIDA?
NOPE.
IT'S SUNNY, KID. YOU SHOULD GO. Y'KNOW, AFTER YOU GET BACK.
OK.
DON'T KNOW WHY YOU'D WANT TO GO *BACK,* THOUGH.
SPACE IS A NEAT PLACE. THAT'S WHY WE STAYED...SET UP THIS TAXI-SERVICE AN' ALL.
SURE YOU WANT TO GO BACK?
I GOTTA.
MY MOM'S GONNA WORRY.
ALRIGHT, THEN. I'M SETTIN' COURSE FOR 1947.
WORMHOLES ARE FUN. YOU'LL SEE. WE GOT 'EM *ALL* FIGURED OUT.

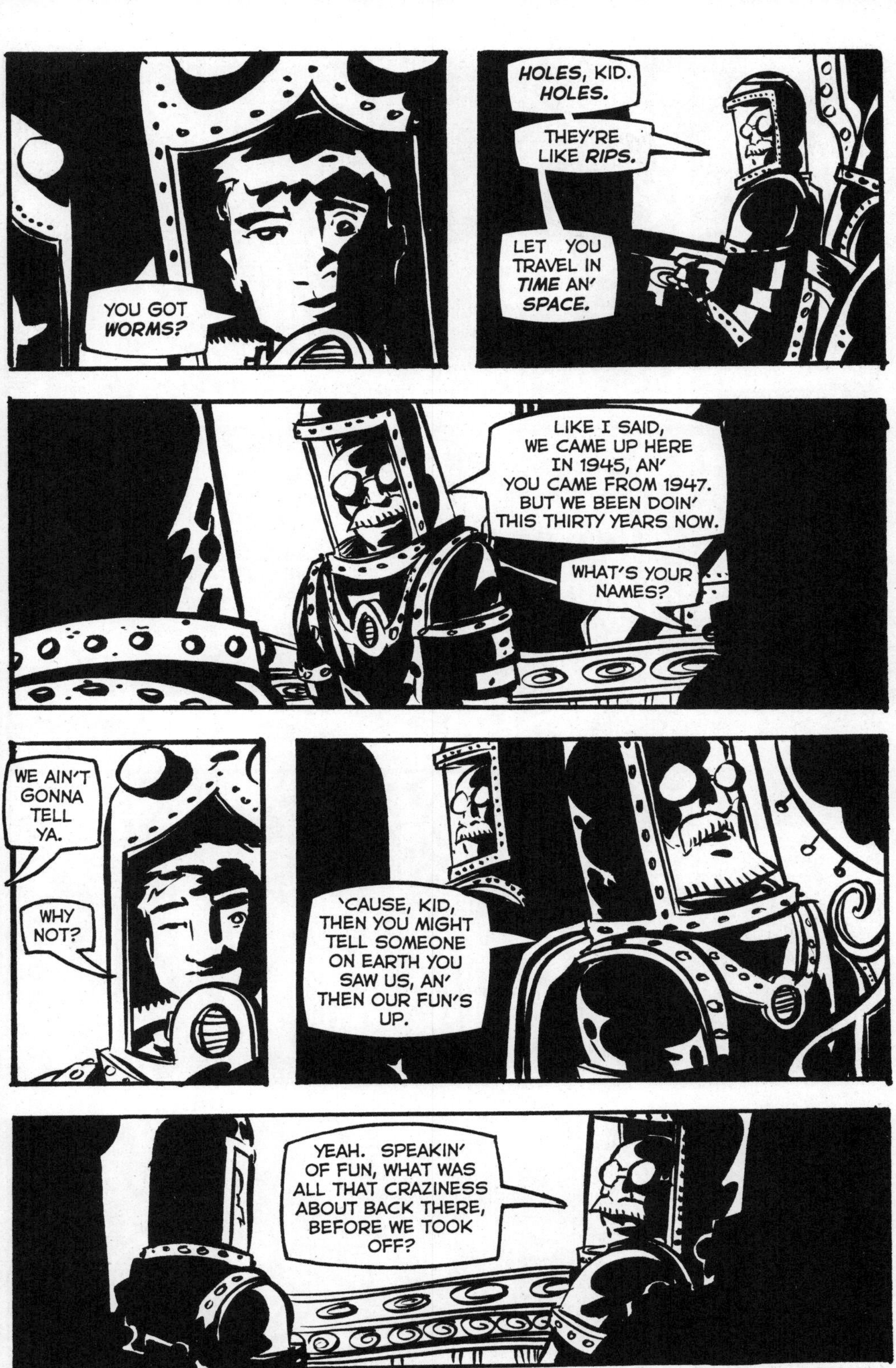
YOU GOT WORMS?
HOLES, KID. HOLES.
THEY'RE LIKE RIPS.
LET YOU TRAVEL IN TIME AN' SPACE.
LIKE I SAID, WE CAME UP HERE IN 1945, AN' YOU CAME FROM 1947. BUT WE BEEN DOIN' THIS THIRTY YEARS NOW.
WHAT'S YOUR NAMES?
WE AIN'T GONNA TELL YA.
WHY NOT?
'CAUSE, KID, THEN YOU MIGHT TELL SOMEONE ON EARTH YOU SAW US, AN' THEN OUR FUN'S UP.
YEAH. SPEAKIN' OF FUN, WHAT WAS ALL THAT CRAZINESS ABOUT BACK THERE, BEFORE WE TOOK OFF?

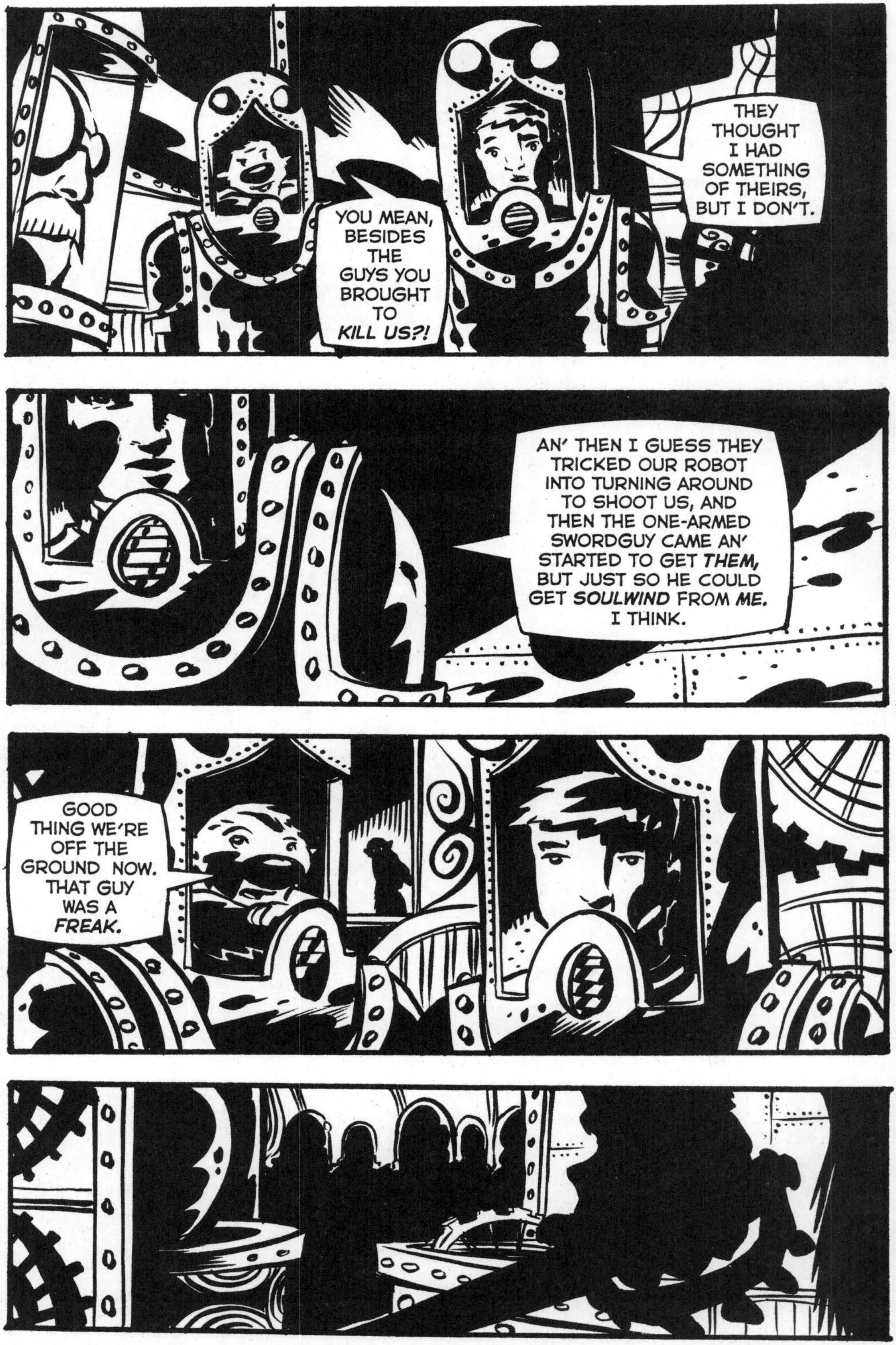

YOU MEAN, BESIDES THE GUYS YOU BROUGHT TO *KILL US?!*
THEY THOUGHT I HAD SOMETHING OF THEIRS, BUT I DON'T.
AN' THEN I GUESS THEY TRICKED OUR ROBOT INTO TURNING AROUND TO SHOOT US, AND THEN THE ONE-ARMED SWORDGUY CAME AN' STARTED TO GET *THEM,* BUT JUST SO HE COULD GET *SOULWIND* FROM *ME.* I THINK.
GOOD THING WE'RE OFF THE GROUND NOW. THAT GUY WAS A *FREAK.*

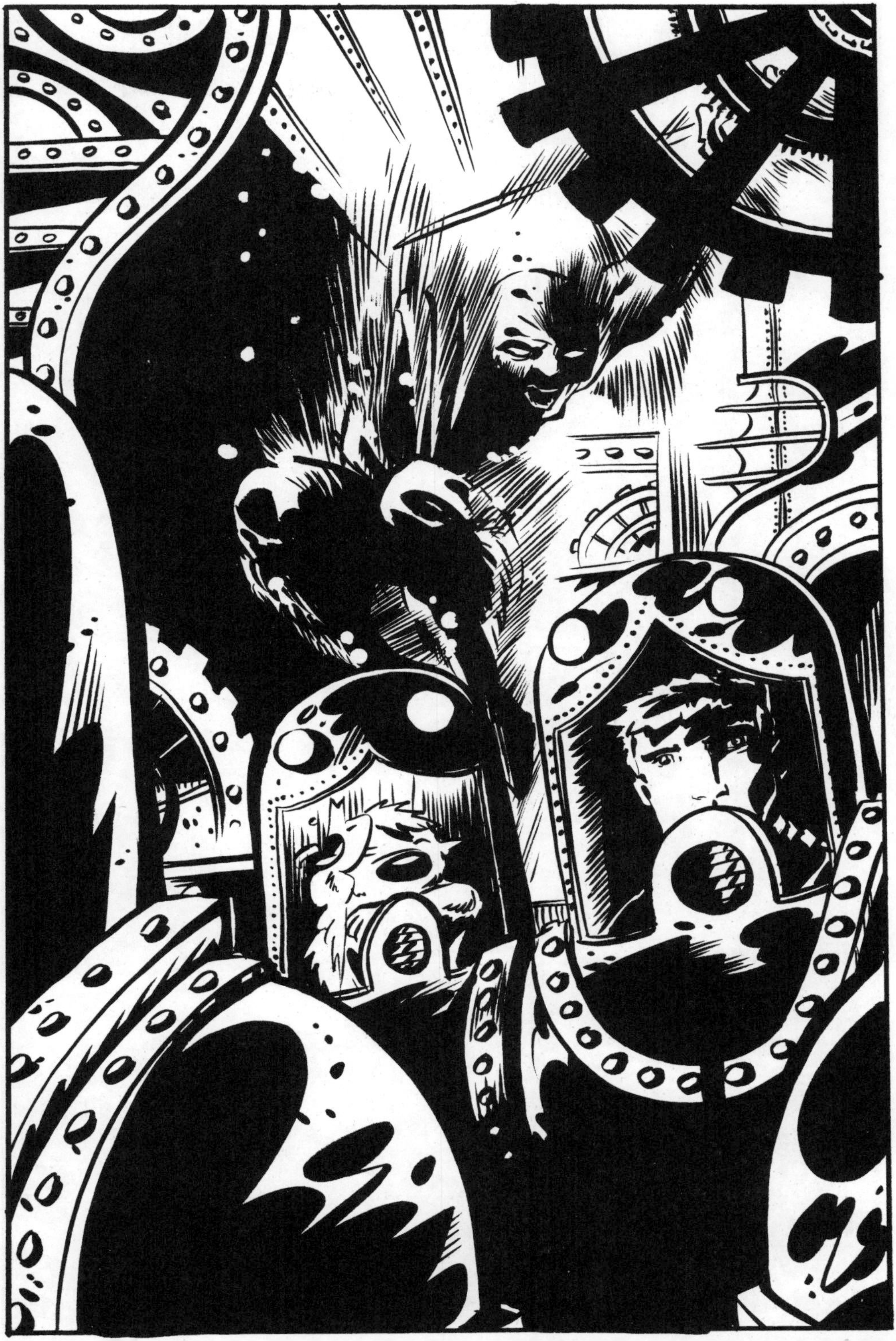

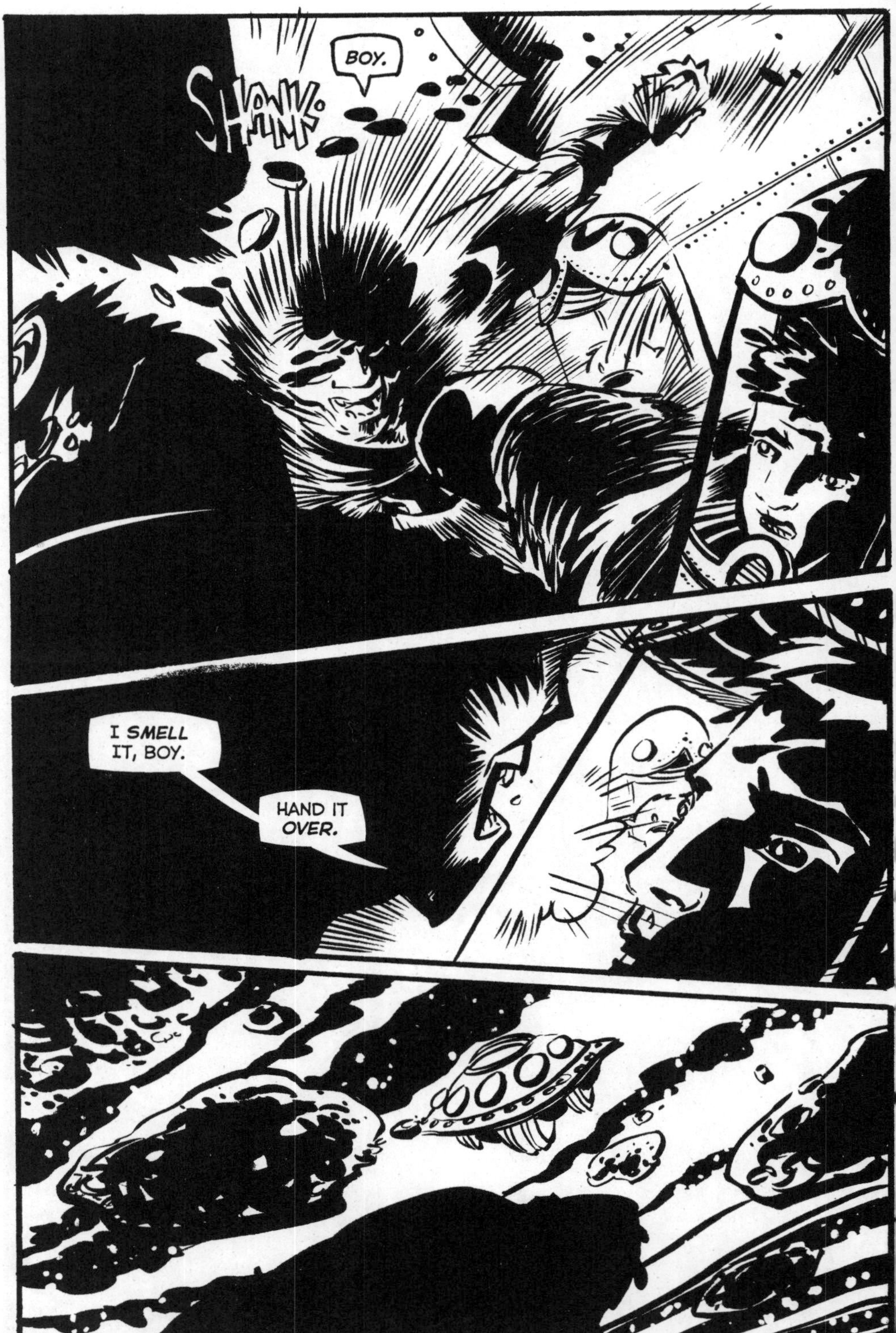
BOY.
SHANK
I SMELL IT, BOY.
HAND IT OVER.

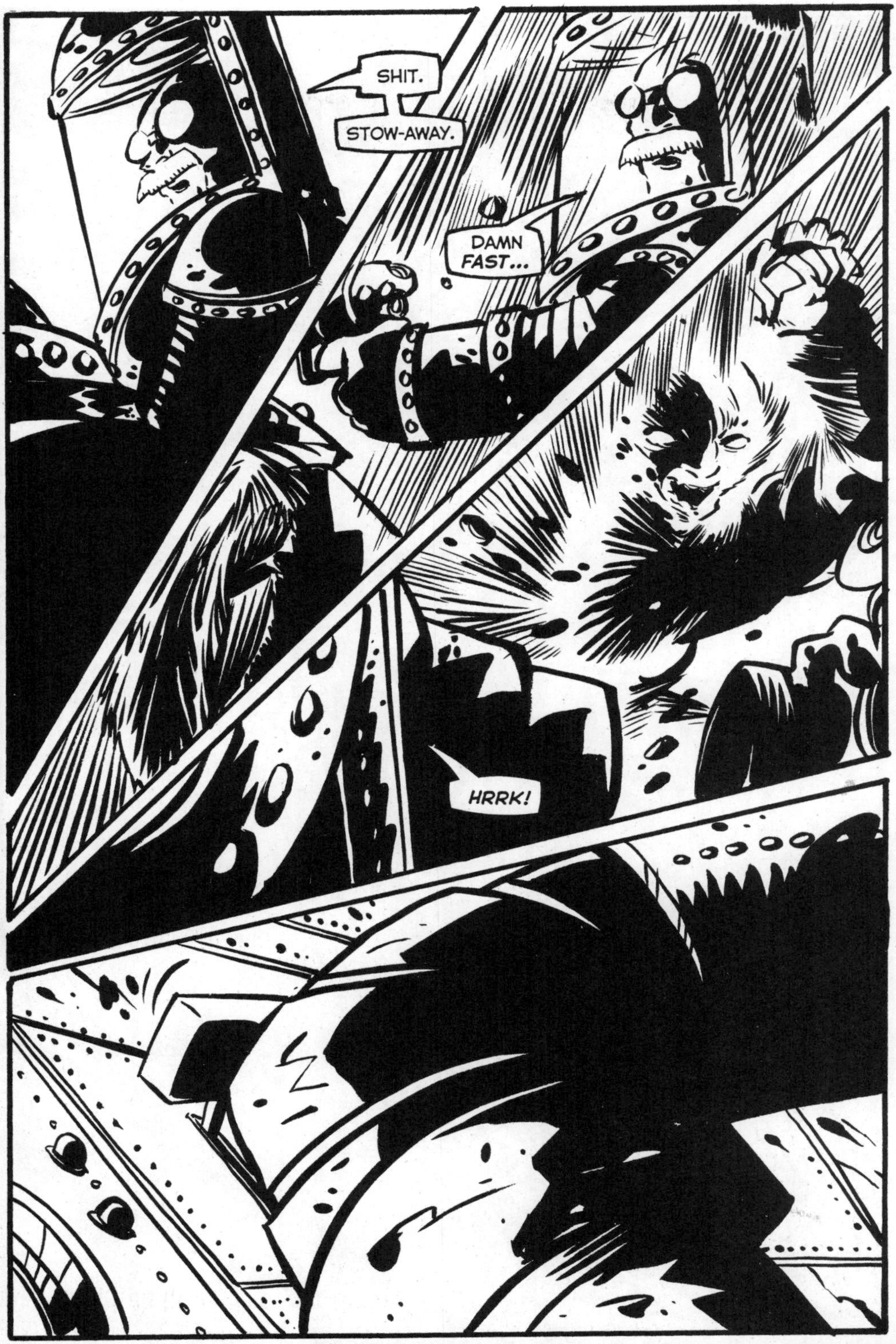
SHIT.
STOW-AWAY.
DAMN FAST...
HRRK!

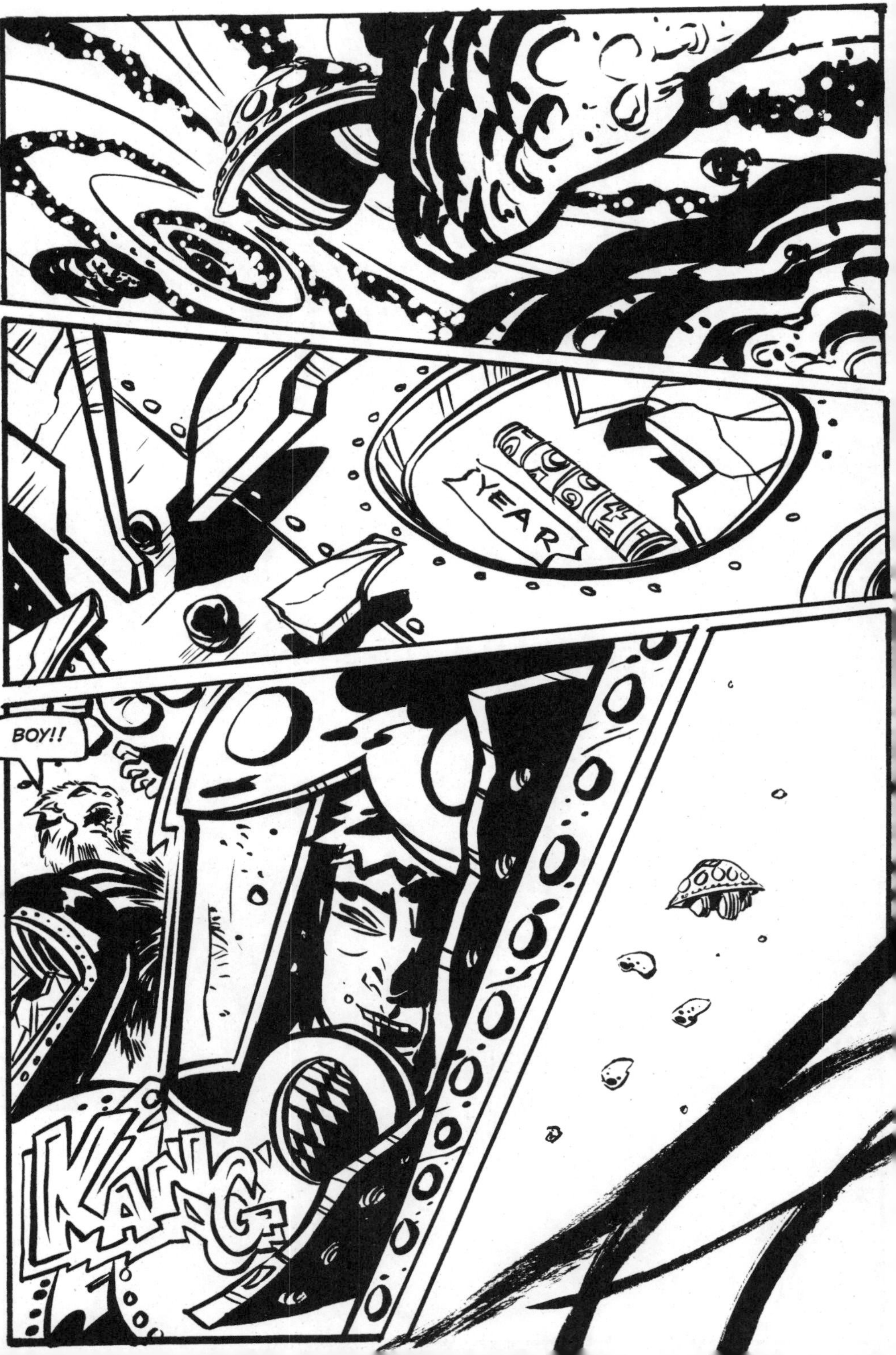
YEAR
BOY!!
KANG

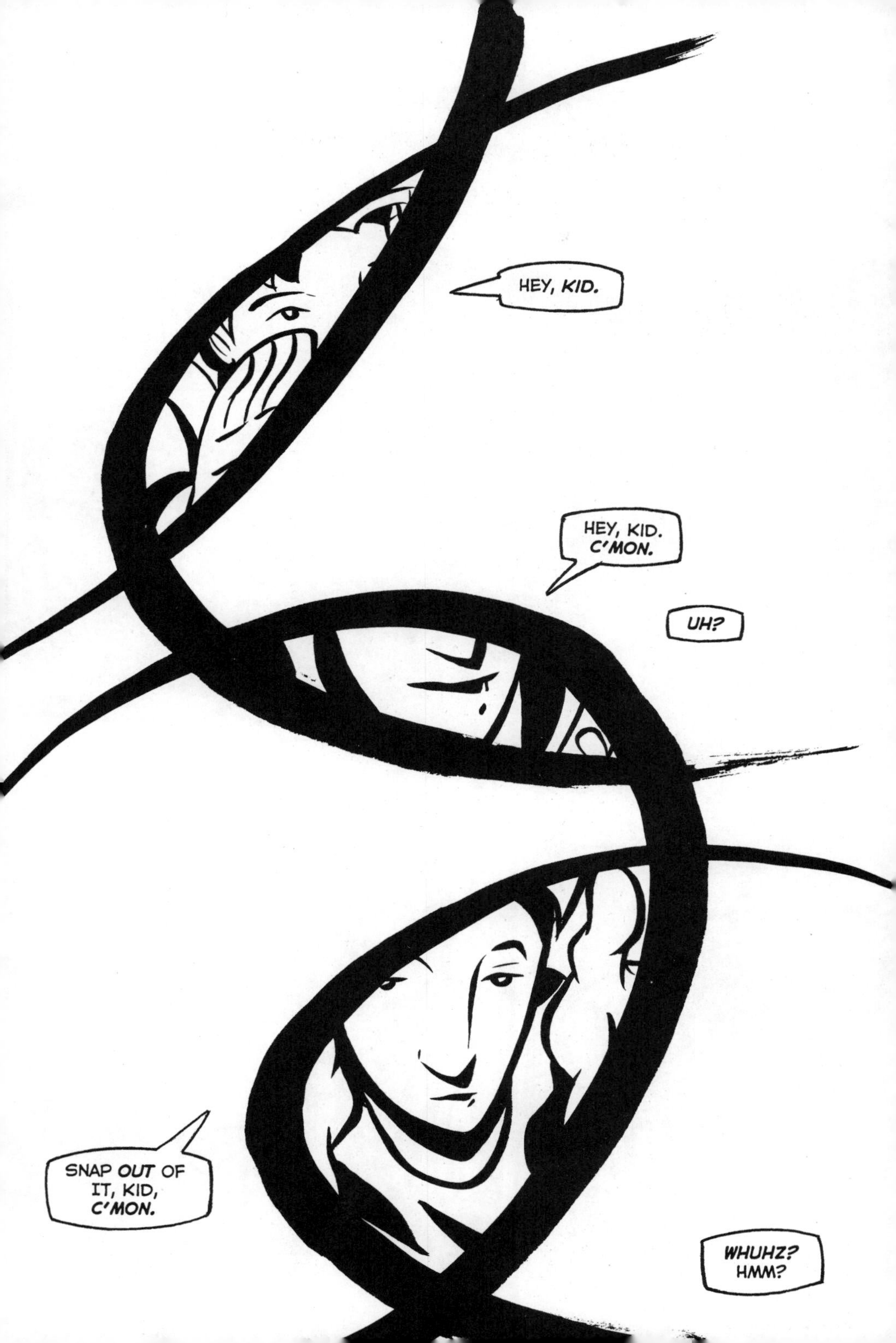
HEY, KID.
HEY, KID. C'MON.
UH?
SNAP OUT OF IT, KID, C'MON.
WHUHZ? HMM?

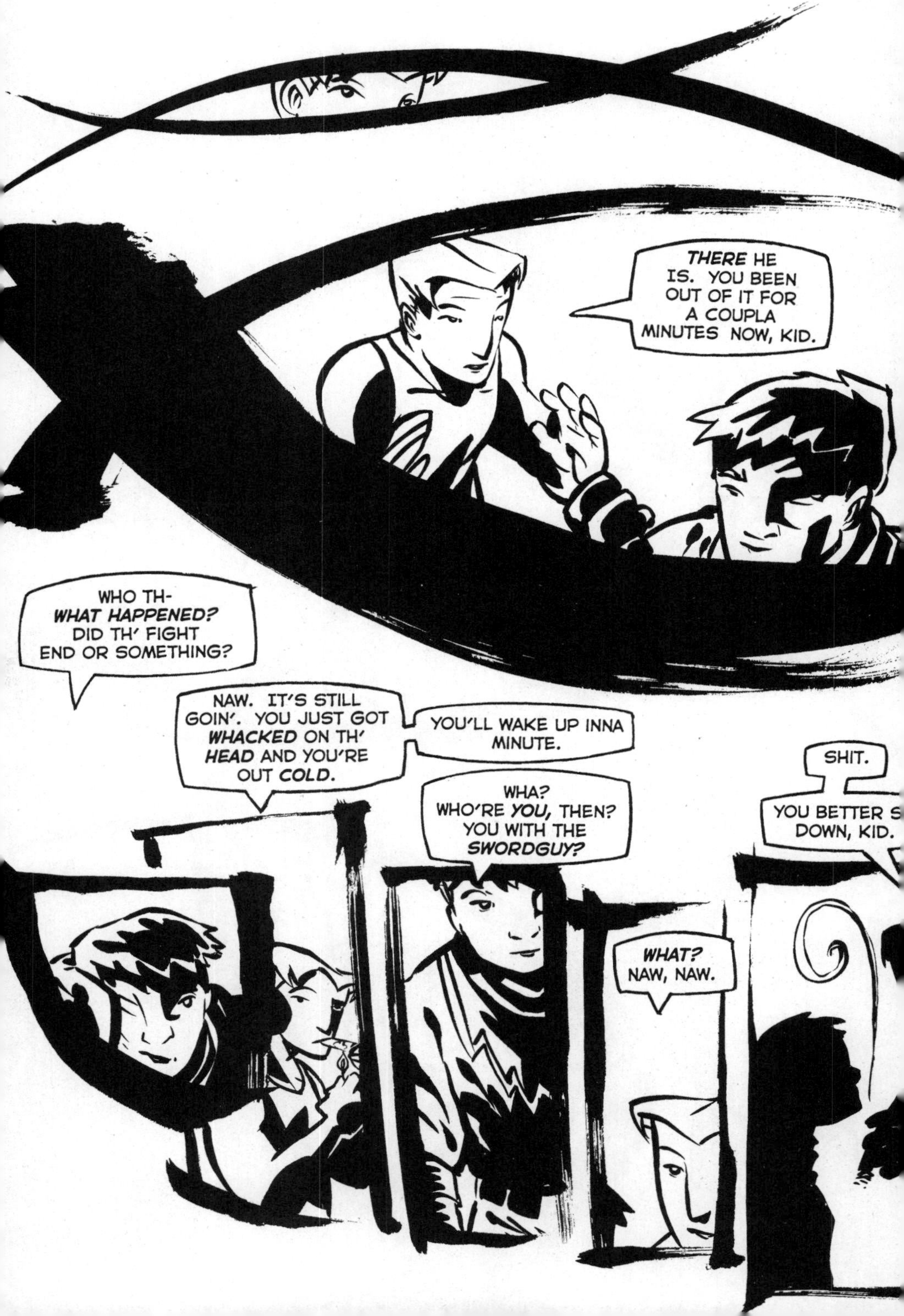

THERE HE IS. YOU BEEN OUT OF IT FOR A COUPLA MINUTES NOW, KID.
WHO TH- *WHAT HAPPENED?* DID TH' FIGHT END OR SOMETHING?
NAW. IT'S STILL GOIN'. YOU JUST GOT *WHACKED* ON TH' *HEAD* AND YOU'RE OUT *COLD*.
YOU'LL WAKE UP INNA MINUTE.
WHA? WHO'RE *YOU,* THEN? YOU WITH THE *SWORDGUY?*
WHAT? NAW, NAW.
SHIT.
YOU BETTER S
DOWN, KID.

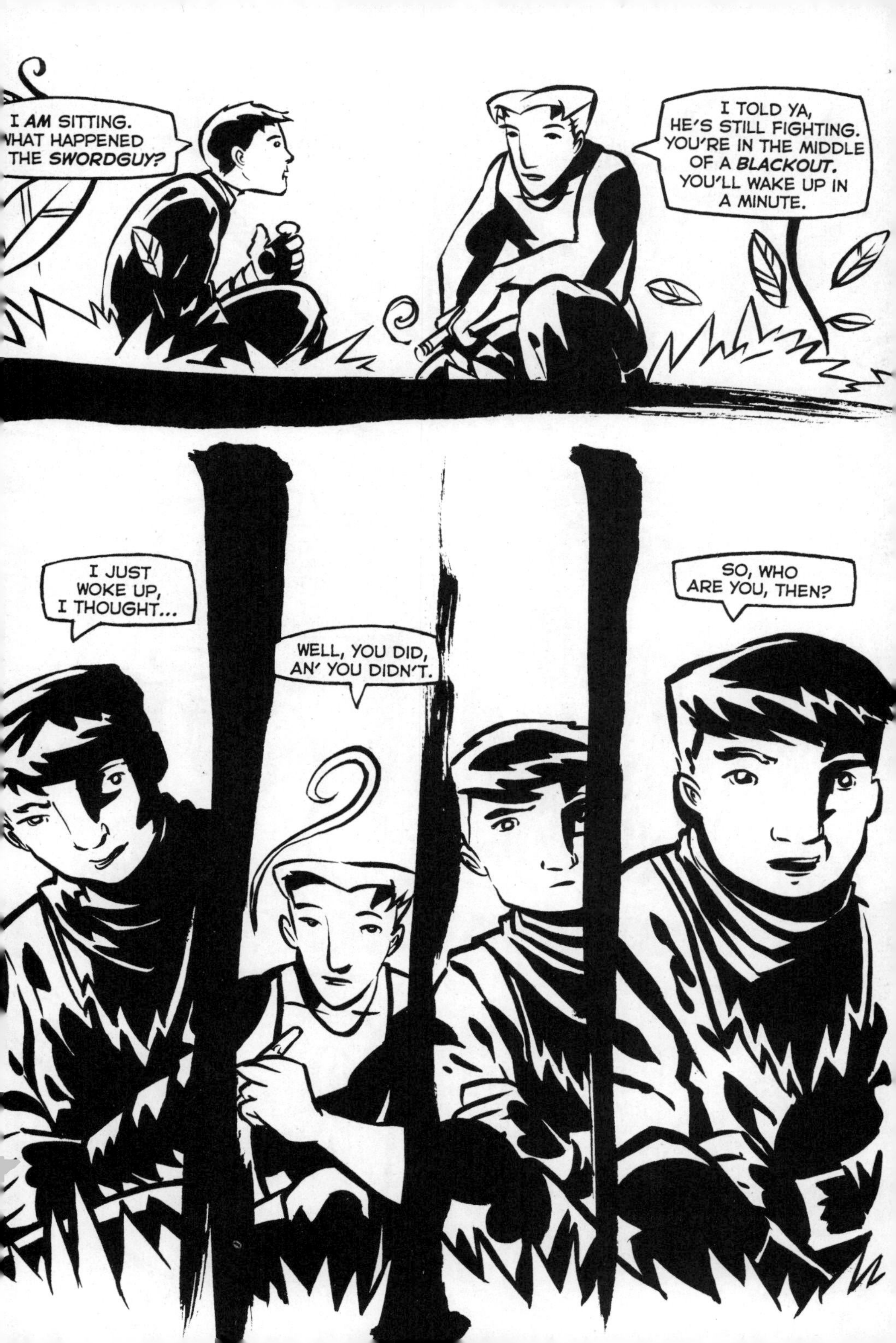

I AM SITTING. WHAT HAPPENED THE SWORDGUY?
I TOLD YA, HE'S STILL FIGHTING. YOU'RE IN THE MIDDLE OF A BLACKOUT. YOU'LL WAKE UP IN A MINUTE.
I JUST WOKE UP, I THOUGHT...
WELL, YOU DID, AN' YOU DIDN'T.
SO, WHO ARE YOU, THEN?

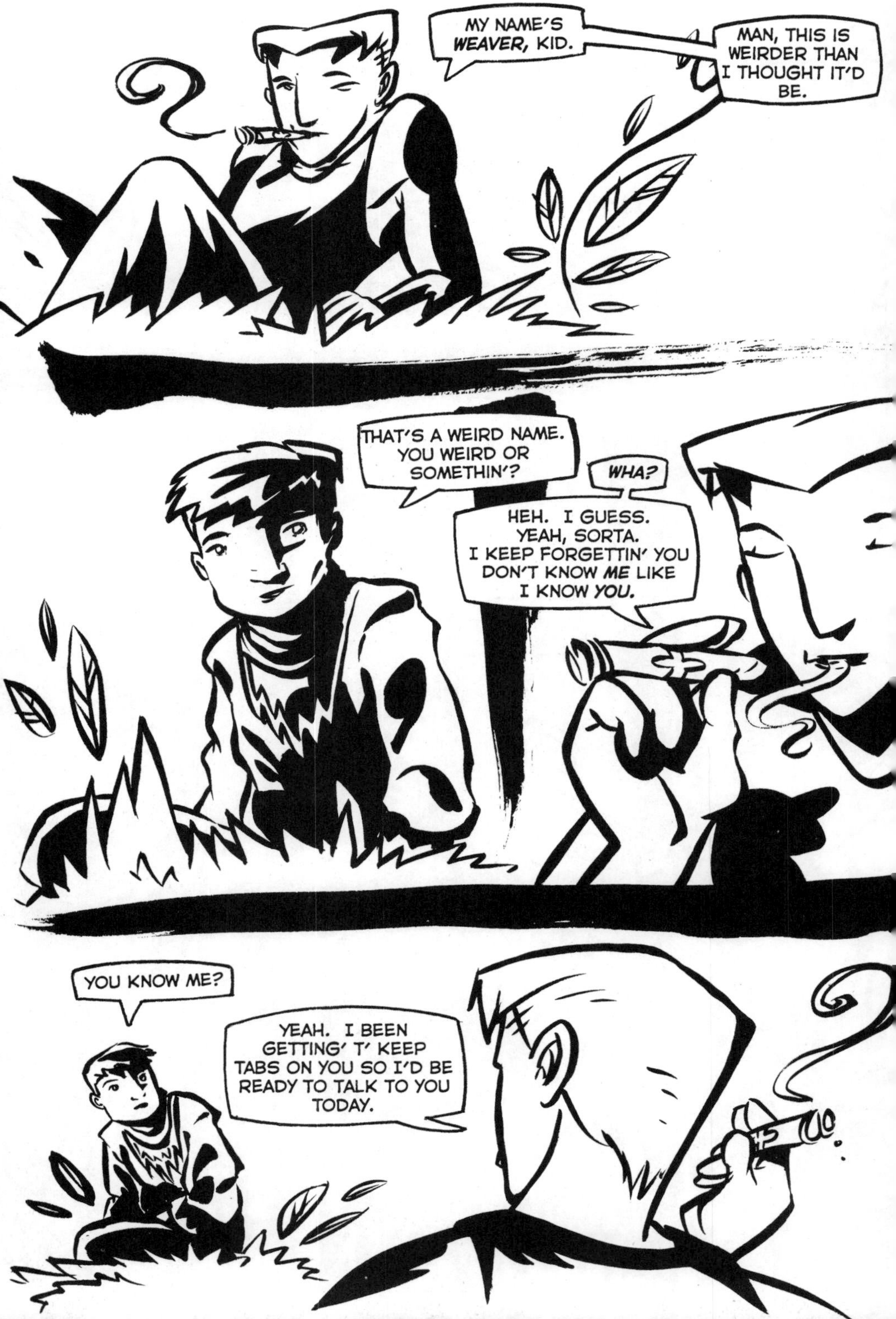
MY NAME'S WEAVER, KID.
MAN, THIS IS WEIRDER THAN I THOUGHT IT'D BE.
THAT'S A WEIRD NAME. YOU WEIRD OR SOMETHIN'?
WHA?
HEH. I GUESS. YEAH, SORTA. I KEEP FORGETTIN' YOU DON'T KNOW ME LIKE I KNOW YOU.
YOU KNOW ME?
YEAH. I BEEN GETTING' T' KEEP TABS ON YOU SO I'D BE READY TO TALK TO YOU TODAY.

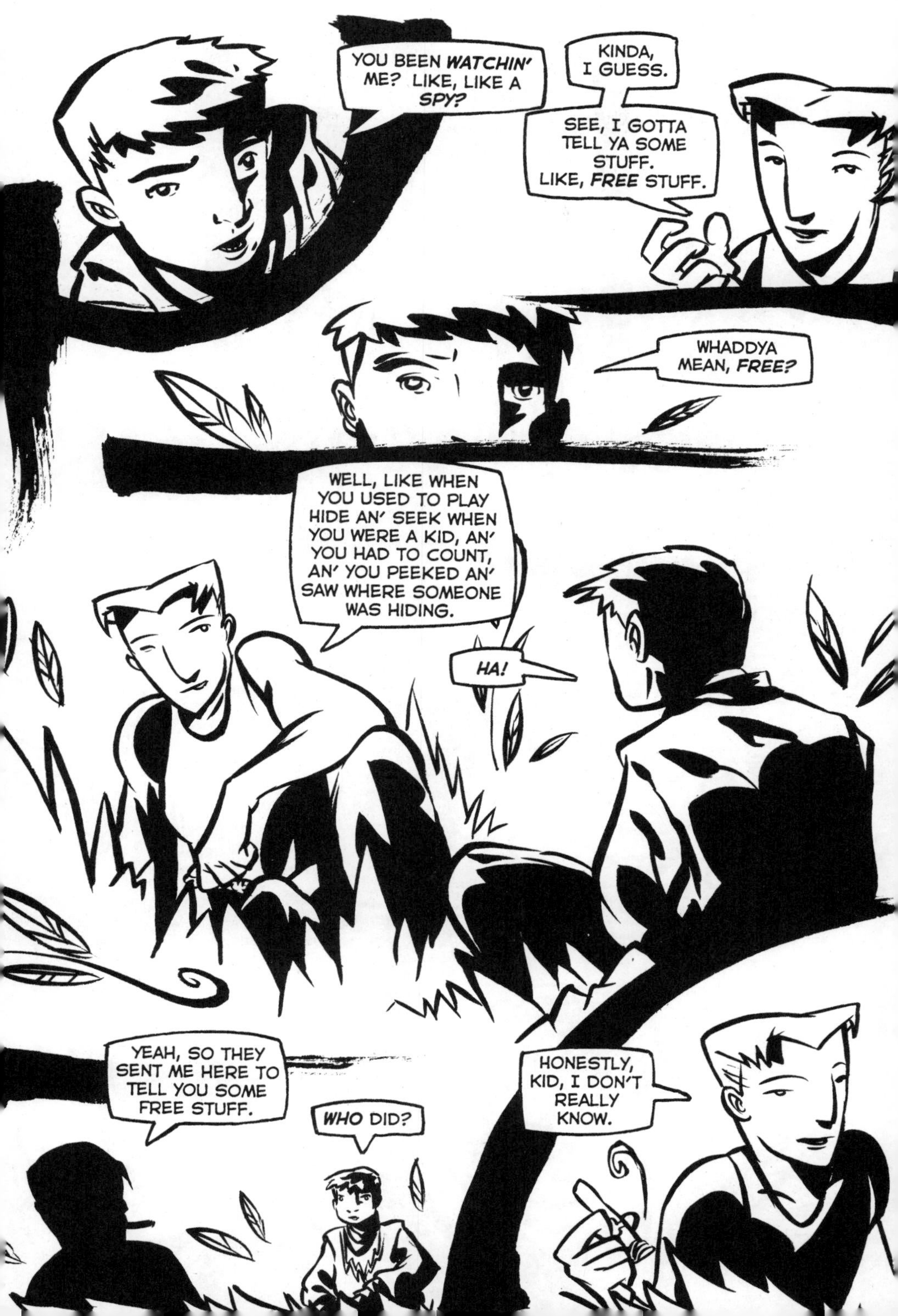

YOU BEEN *WATCHIN'* ME? LIKE, LIKE A *SPY?*
KINDA, I GUESS.
SEE, I GOTTA TELL YA SOME STUFF. LIKE, *FREE* STUFF.
WHADDYA MEAN, *FREE?*
WELL, LIKE WHEN YOU USED TO PLAY HIDE AN' SEEK WHEN YOU WERE A KID, AN' YOU HAD TO COUNT, AN' YOU PEEKED AN' SAW WHERE SOMEONE WAS HIDING.
HA!
YEAH, SO THEY SENT ME HERE TO TELL YOU SOME FREE STUFF.
WHO DID?
HONESTLY, KID, I DON'T REALLY KNOW.

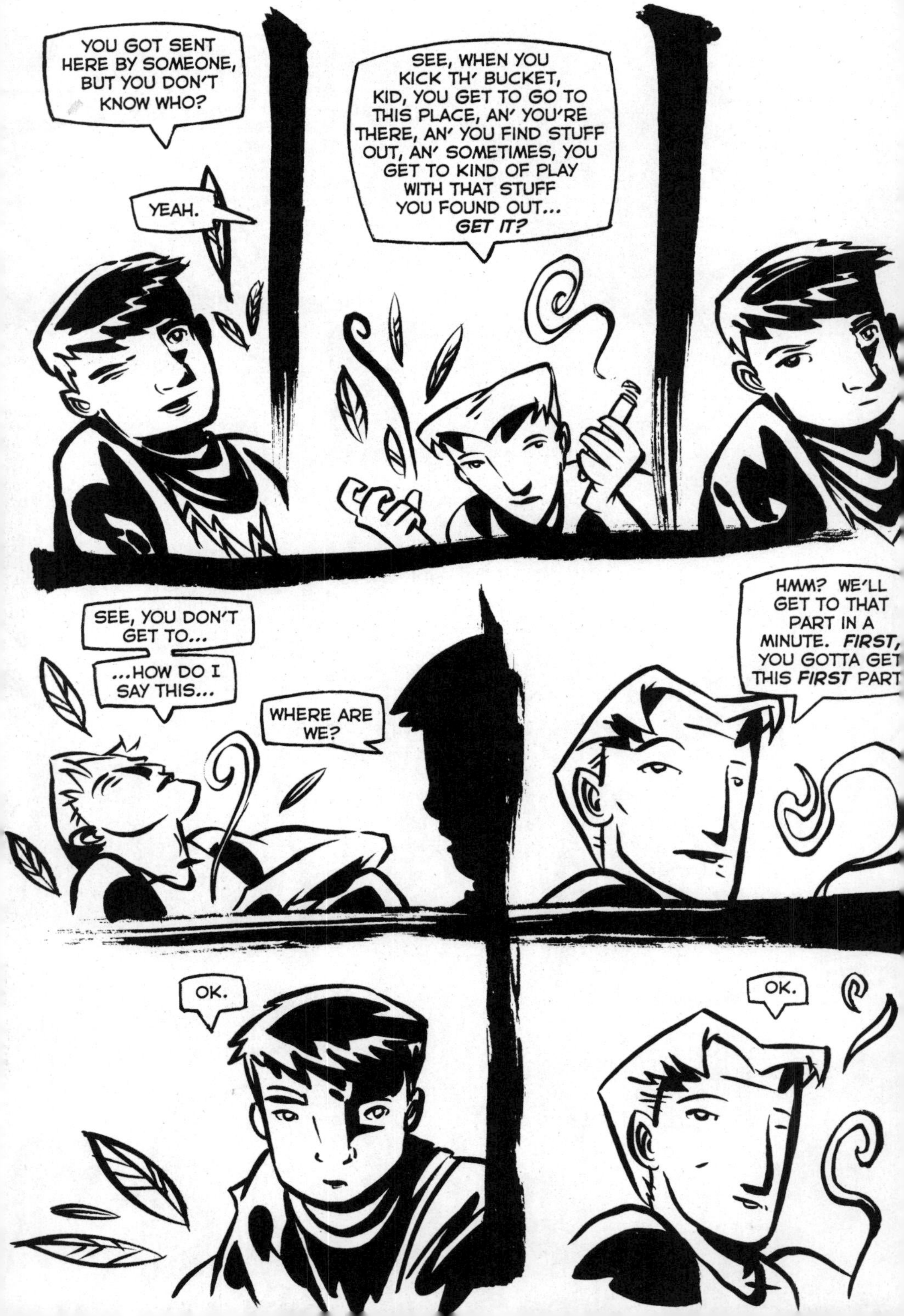
YOU GOT SENT HERE BY SOMEONE, BUT YOU DON'T KNOW WHO?
YEAH.
SEE, WHEN YOU KICK TH' BUCKET, KID, YOU GET TO GO TO THIS PLACE, AN' YOU'RE THERE, AN' YOU FIND STUFF OUT, AN' SOMETIMES, YOU GET TO KIND OF PLAY WITH THAT STUFF YOU FOUND OUT... *GET IT?*
SEE, YOU DON'T GET TO...
...HOW DO I SAY THIS...
WHERE ARE WE?
HMM? WE'LL GET TO THAT PART IN A MINUTE. *FIRST,* YOU GOTTA GET THIS *FIRST* PART
OK.
OK.

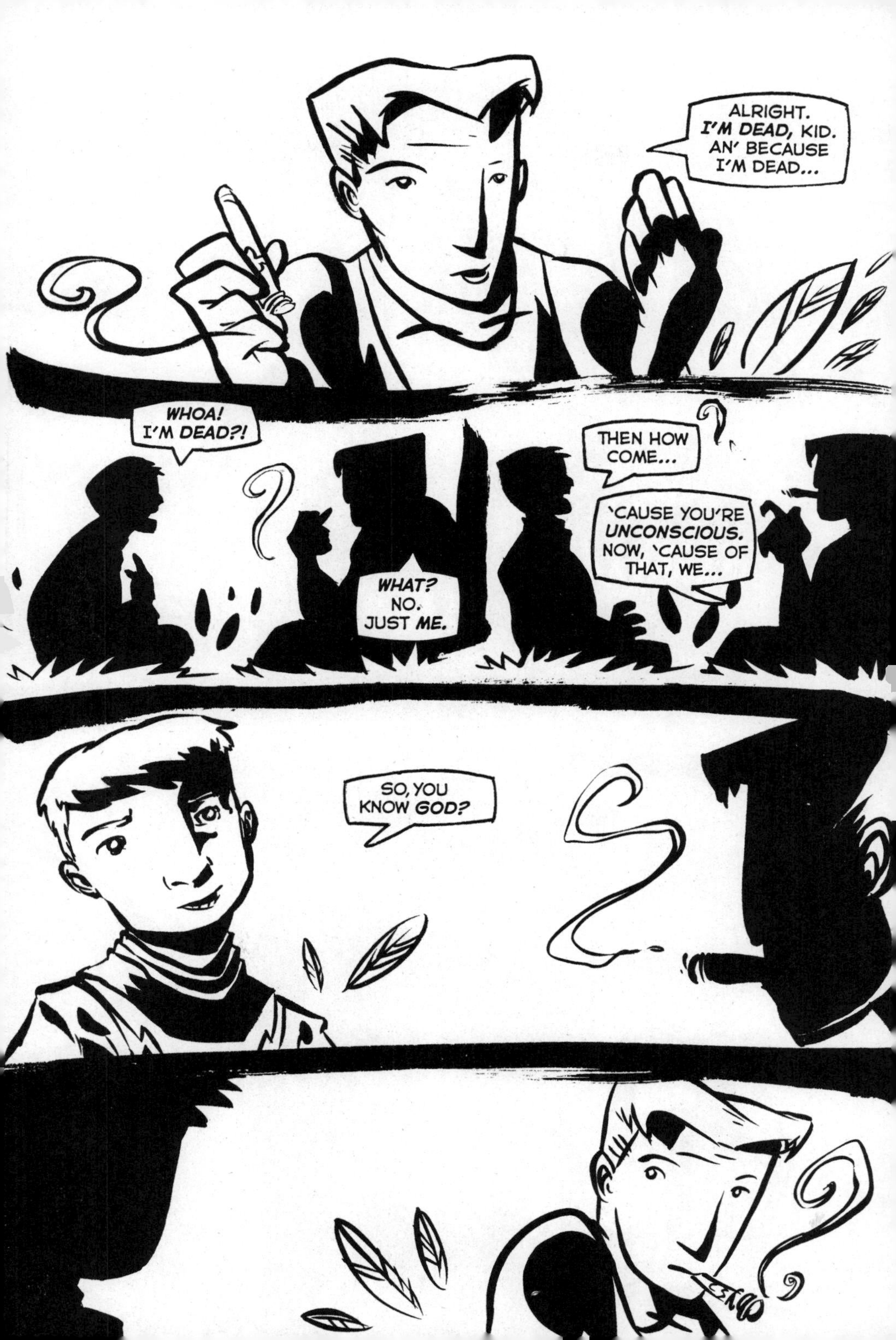
ALRIGHT. I'M DEAD, KID. AN' BECAUSE I'M DEAD...
WHOA! I'M DEAD?!
WHAT? NO. JUST ME.
THEN HOW COME...
'CAUSE YOU'RE UNCONSCIOUS. NOW, 'CAUSE OF THAT, WE...
SO, YOU KNOW GOD?

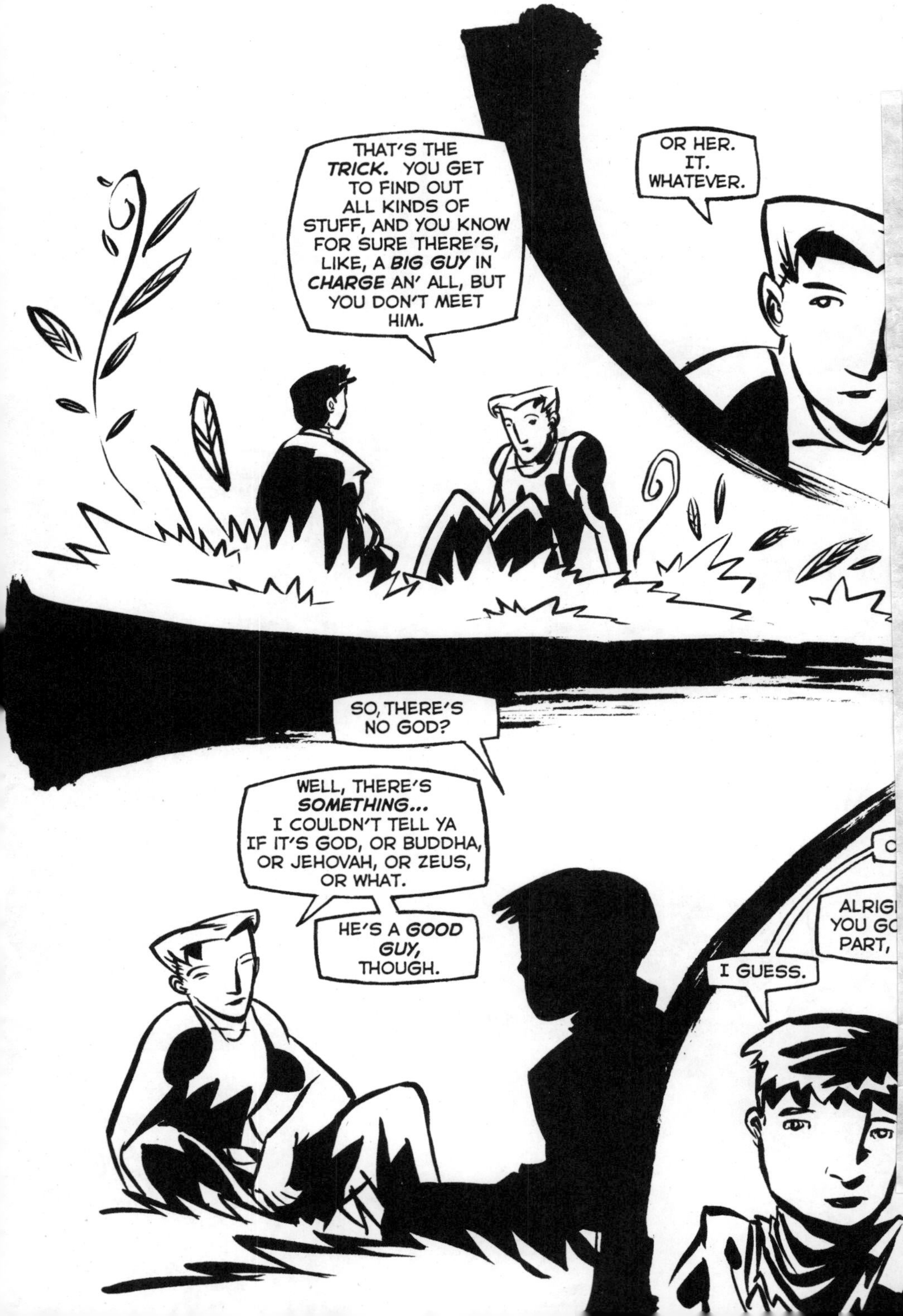
THAT'S THE *TRICK.* YOU GET TO FIND OUT ALL KINDS OF STUFF, AND YOU KNOW FOR SURE THERE'S, LIKE, A *BIG GUY* IN *CHARGE* AN' ALL, BUT YOU DON'T MEET HIM.
OR HER. IT. WHATEVER.
SO, THERE'S NO GOD?
WELL, THERE'S *SOMETHING...* I COULDN'T TELL YA IF IT'S GOD, OR BUDDHA, OR JEHOVAH, OR ZEUS, OR WHAT.
HE'S A *GOOD GUY,* THOUGH.
I GUESS.

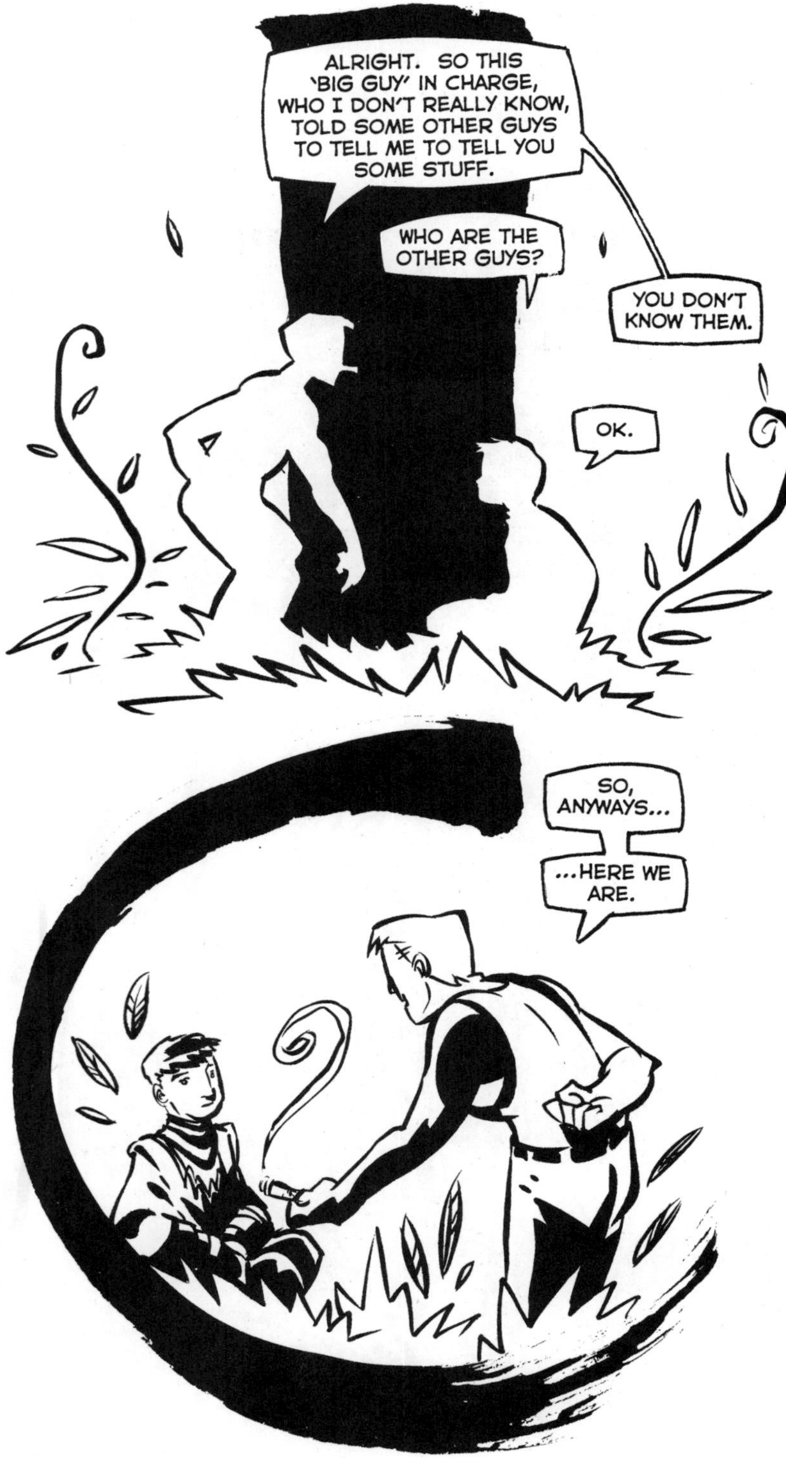
ALRIGHT. SO THIS 'BIG GUY' IN CHARGE, WHO I DON'T REALLY KNOW, TOLD SOME OTHER GUYS TO TELL ME TO TELL YOU SOME STUFF.
WHO ARE THE OTHER GUYS?
YOU DON'T KNOW THEM.
OK.
SO, ANYWAYS...
...HERE WE ARE.

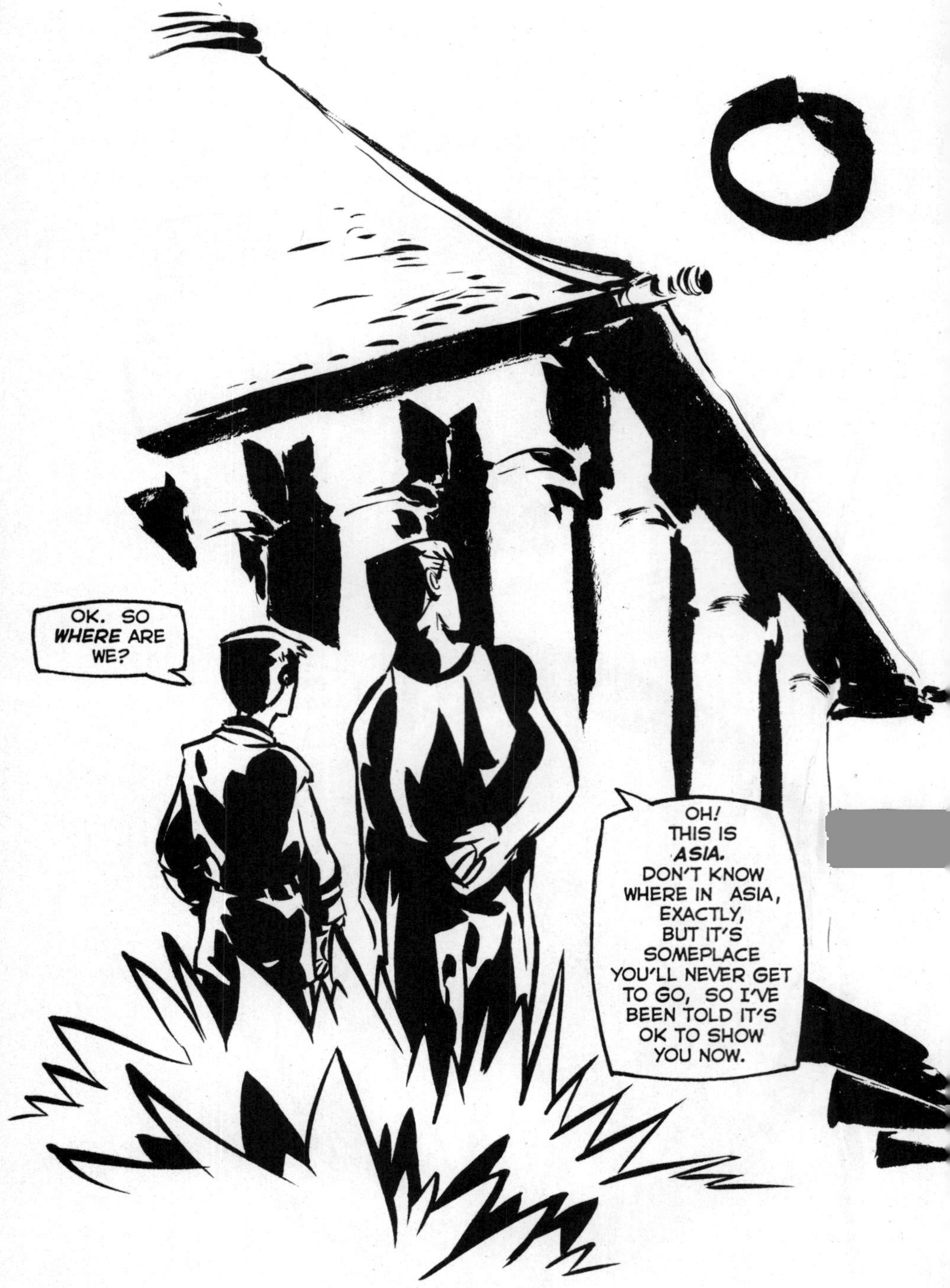
OK. SO *WHERE* ARE WE?
OH! THIS IS *ASIA.* DON'T KNOW WHERE IN ASIA, EXACTLY, BUT IT'S SOMEPLACE YOU'LL NEVER GET TO GO, SO I'VE BEEN TOLD IT'S OK TO SHOW YOU NOW.

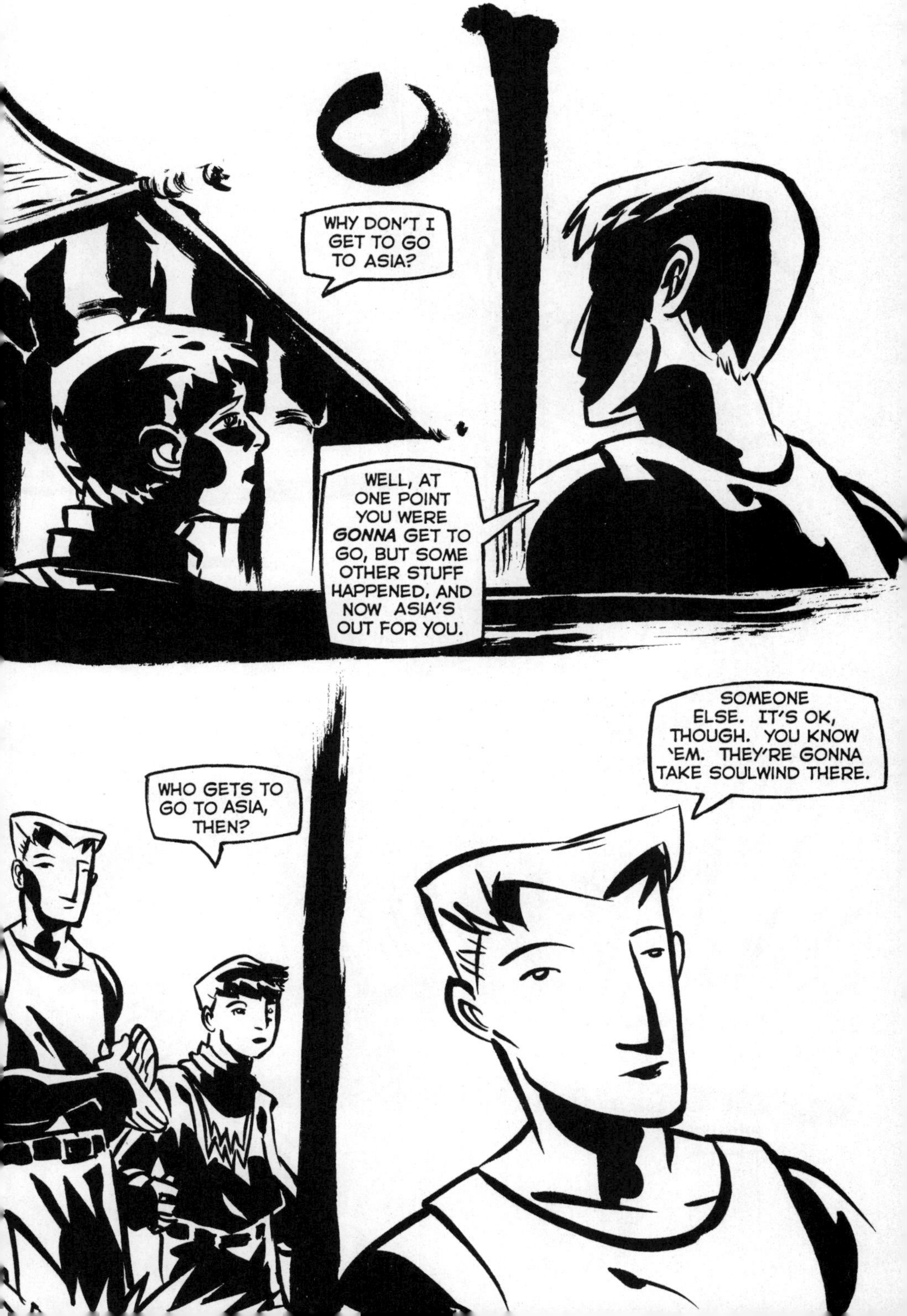
WHY DON'T I GET TO GO TO ASIA?
WELL, AT ONE POINT YOU WERE *GONNA* GET TO GO, BUT SOME OTHER STUFF HAPPENED, AND NOW ASIA'S OUT FOR YOU.
WHO GETS TO GO TO ASIA, THEN?
SOMEONE ELSE. IT'S OK, THOUGH. YOU KNOW 'EM. THEY'RE GONNA TAKE SOULWIND THERE.

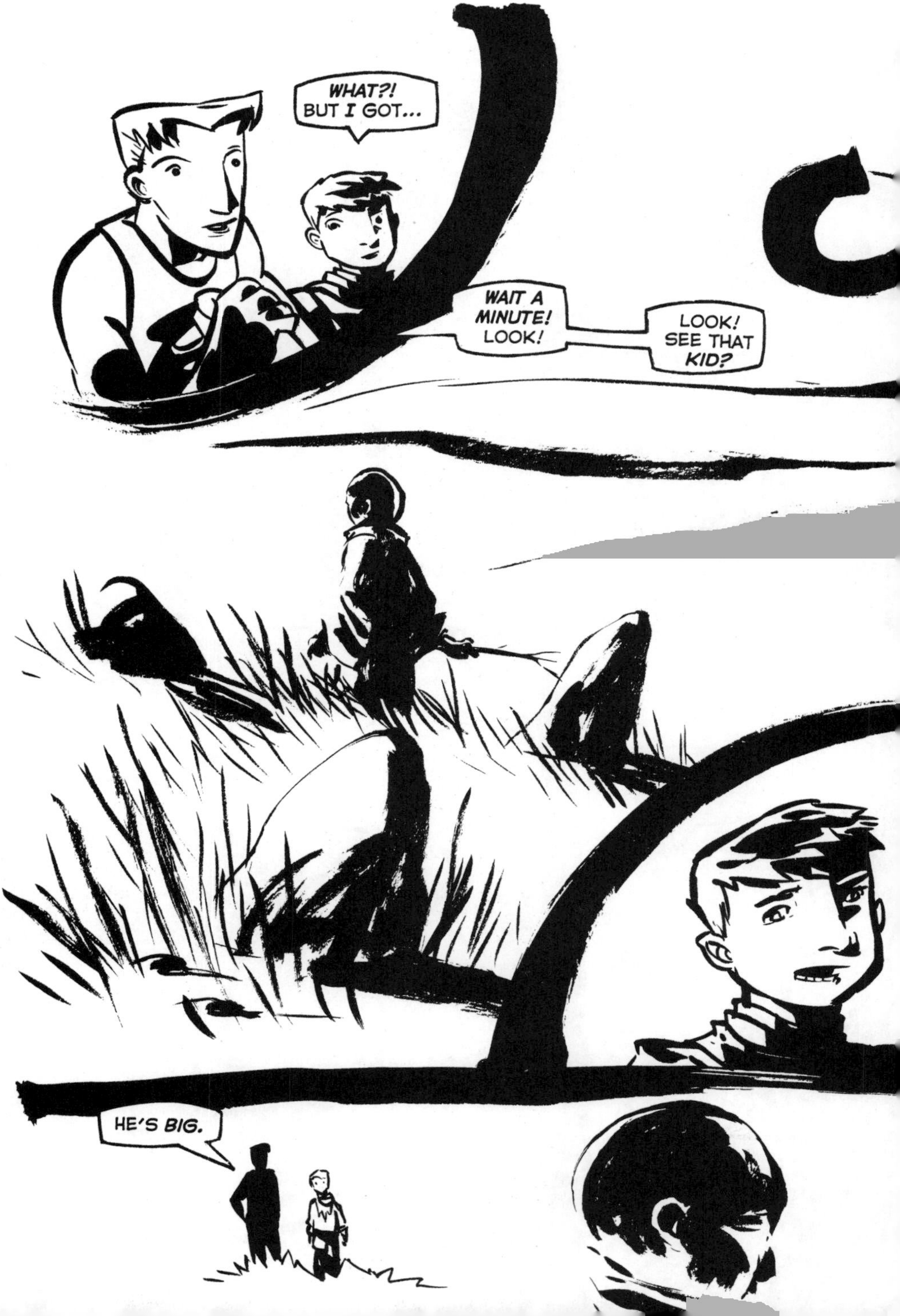
WHAT?! BUT I GOT...
WAIT A MINUTE! LOOK!
LOOK! SEE THAT KID?
HE'S BIG.

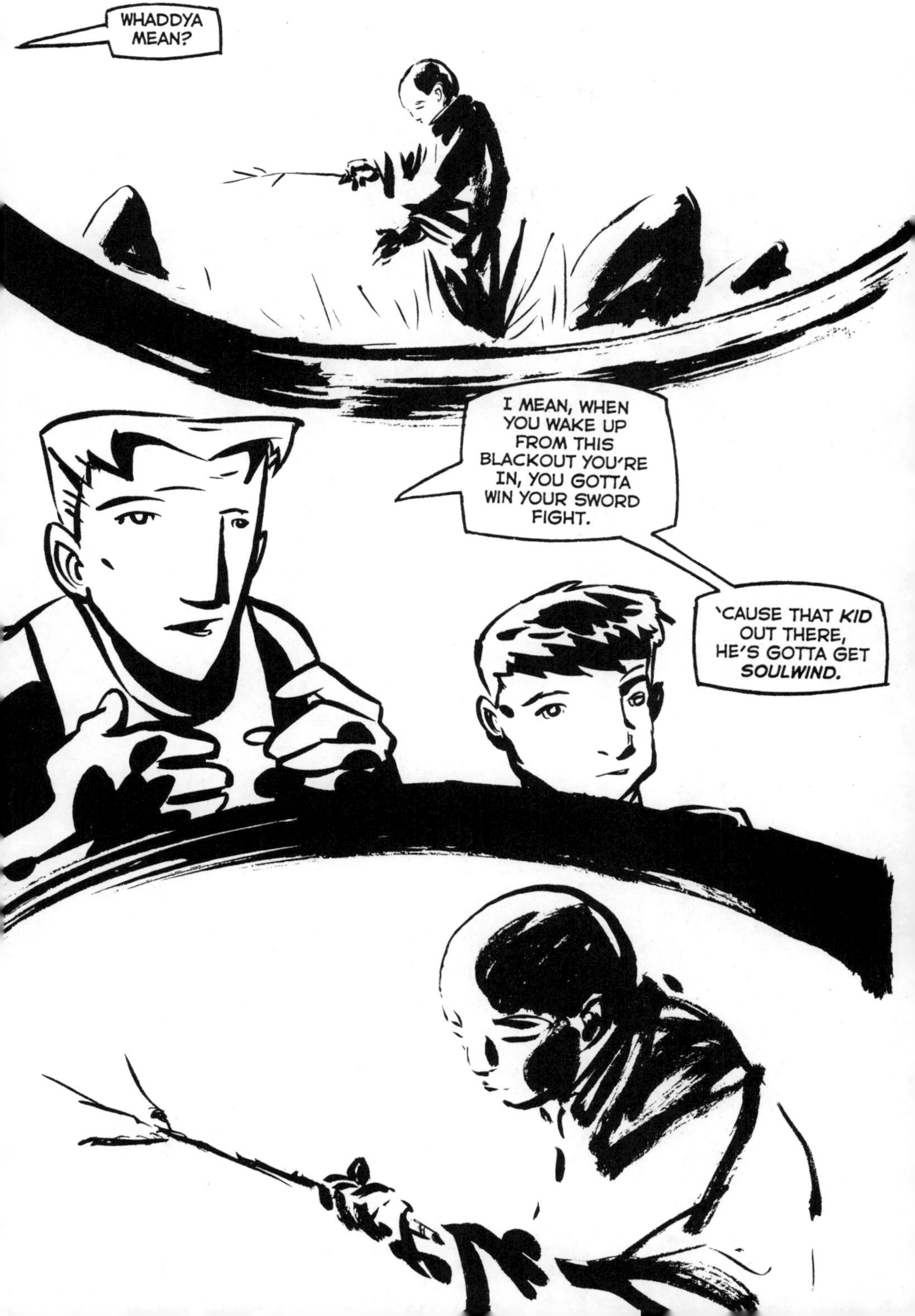
WHADDYA MEAN?
I MEAN, WHEN YOU WAKE UP FROM THIS BLACKOUT YOU'RE IN, YOU GOTTA WIN YOUR SWORD FIGHT.
'CAUSE THAT *KID* OUT THERE, HE'S GOTTA GET *SOULWIND.*

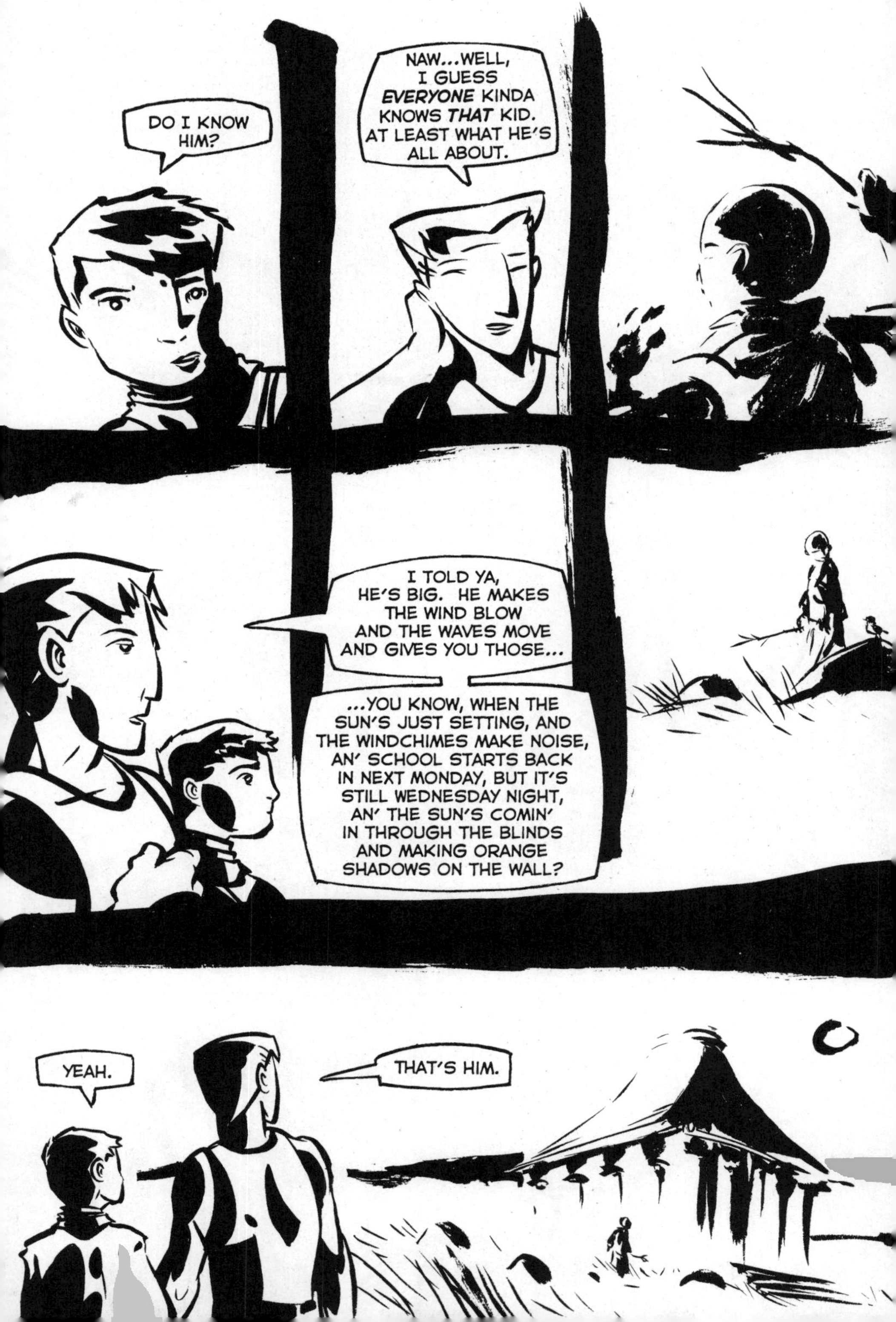
DO I KNOW HIM?
NAW...WELL, I GUESS *EVERYONE* KINDA KNOWS *THAT* KID. AT LEAST WHAT HE'S ALL ABOUT.
I TOLD YA, HE'S BIG. HE MAKES THE WIND BLOW AND THE WAVES MOVE AND GIVES YOU THOSE...
...YOU KNOW, WHEN THE SUN'S JUST SETTING, AND THE WINDCHIMES MAKE NOISE, AN' SCHOOL STARTS BACK IN NEXT MONDAY, BUT IT'S STILL WEDNESDAY NIGHT, AN' THE SUN'S COMIN' IN THROUGH THE BLINDS AND MAKING ORANGE SHADOWS ON THE WALL?
YEAH.
THAT'S HIM.

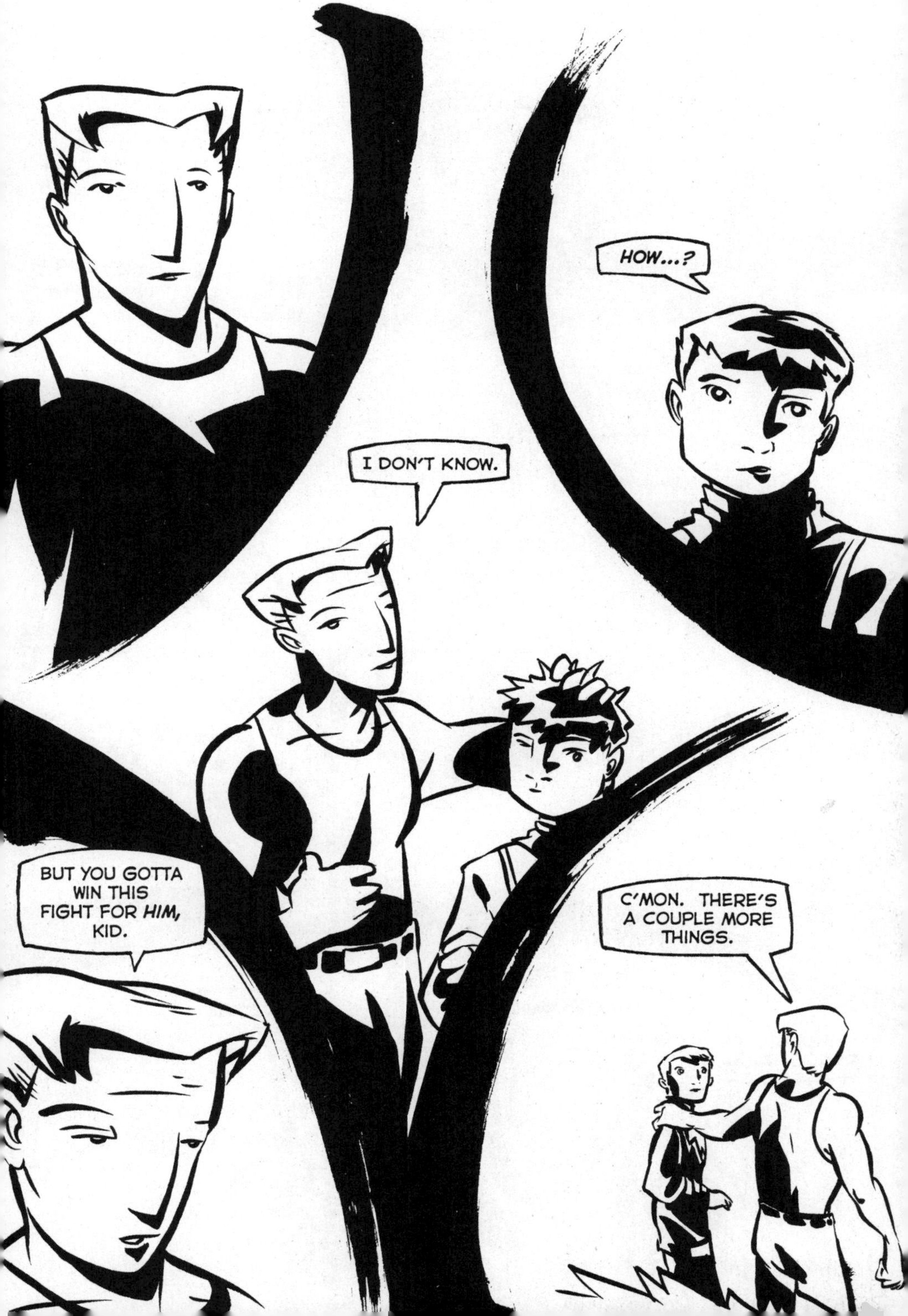
HOW...?
I DON'T KNOW.
BUT YOU GOTTA WIN THIS FIGHT FOR *HIM*, KID.
C'MON. THERE'S A COUPLE MORE THINGS.

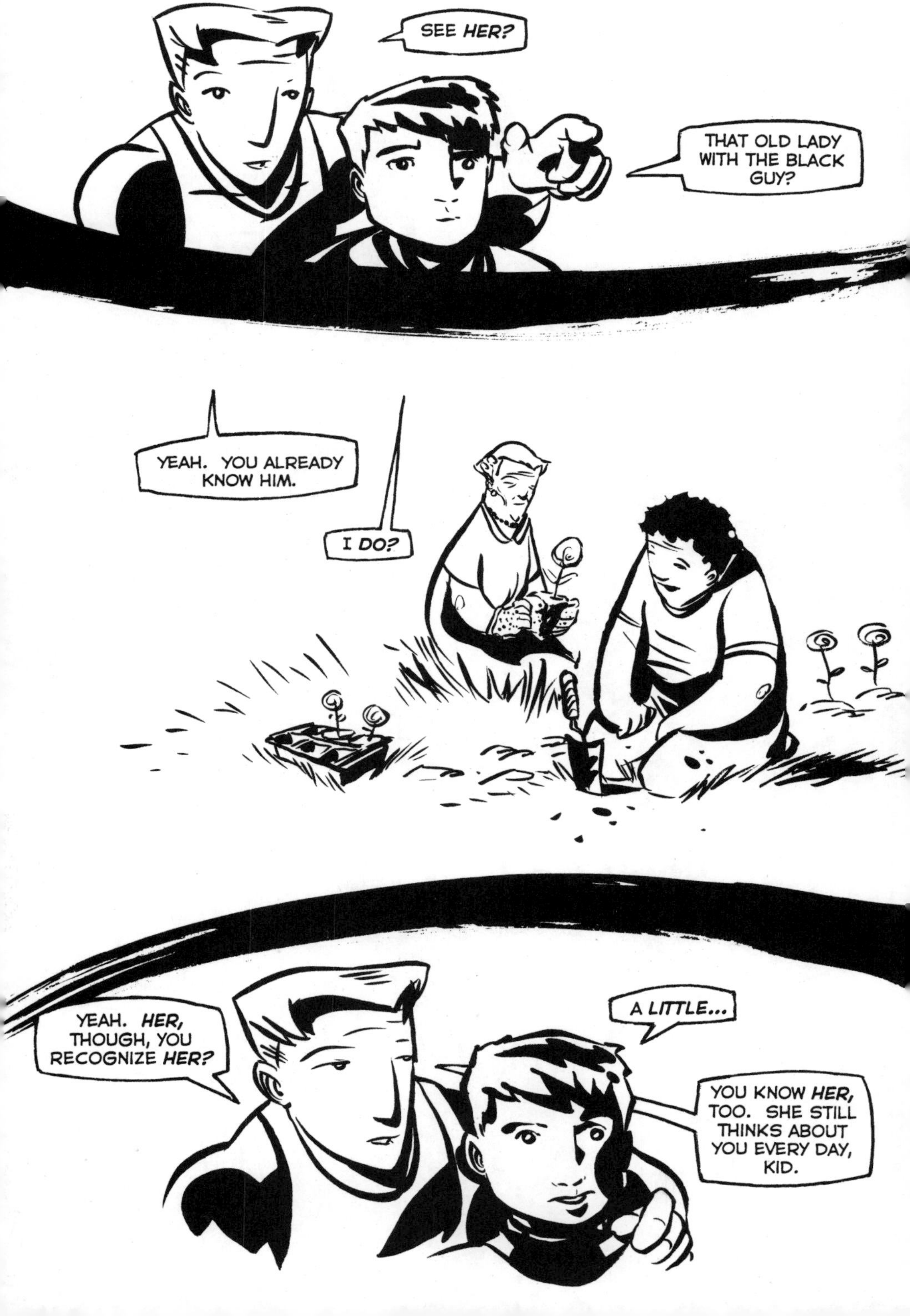

SEE *HER?*
THAT OLD LADY WITH THE BLACK GUY?
YEAH. YOU ALREADY KNOW HIM.
I *DO?*
YEAH. *HER,* THOUGH, YOU RECOGNIZE *HER?*
A *LITTLE...*
YOU KNOW *HER,* TOO. SHE STILL THINKS ABOUT YOU EVERY DAY, KID.

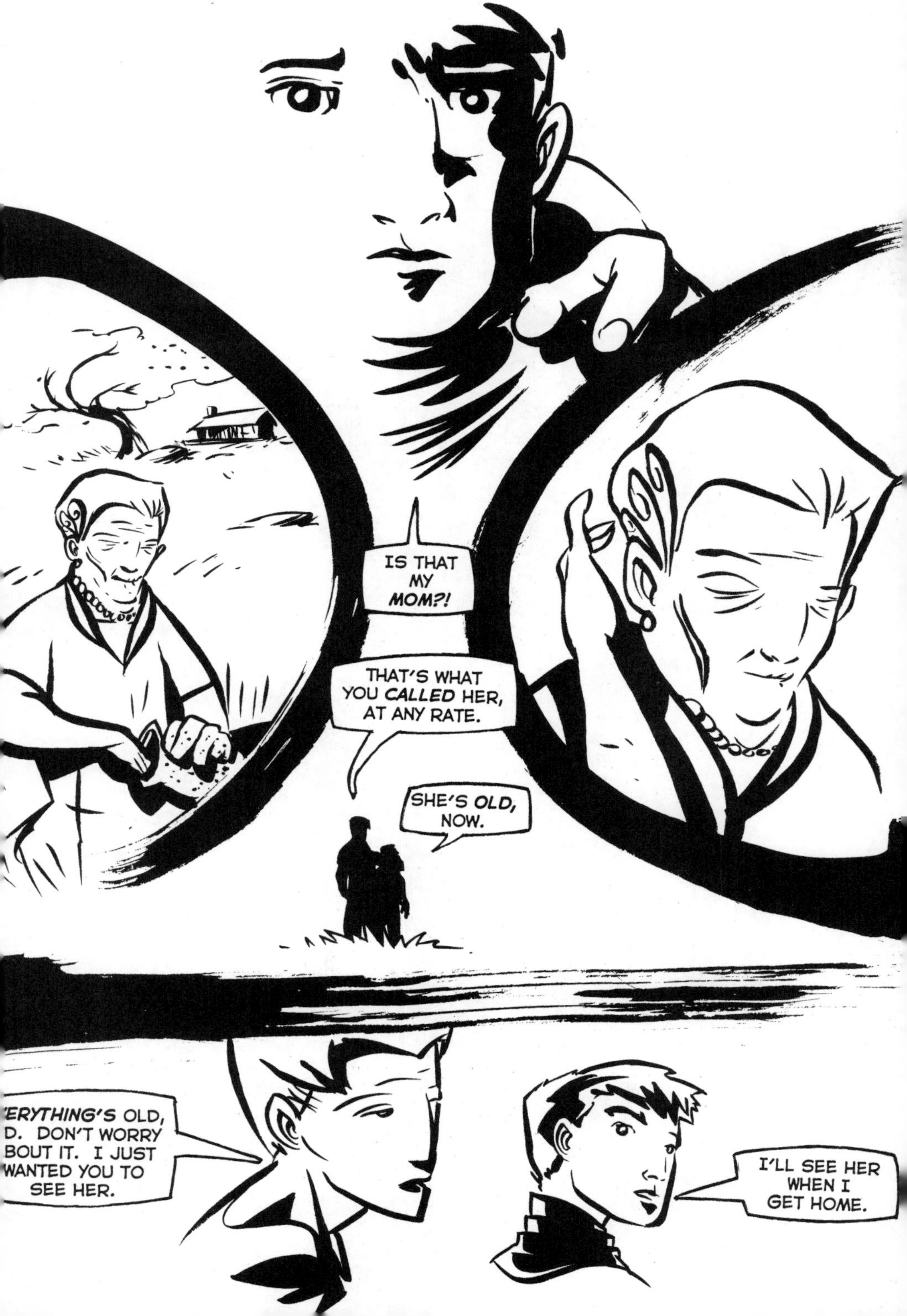

IS THAT MY *MOM?!*
THAT'S WHAT YOU *CALLED* HER, AT ANY RATE.
SHE'S *OLD,* NOW.
ERYTHING'S OLD, D. DON'T WORRY BOUT IT. I JUST WANTED YOU TO SEE HER.
I'LL SEE HER WHEN I GET HOME.

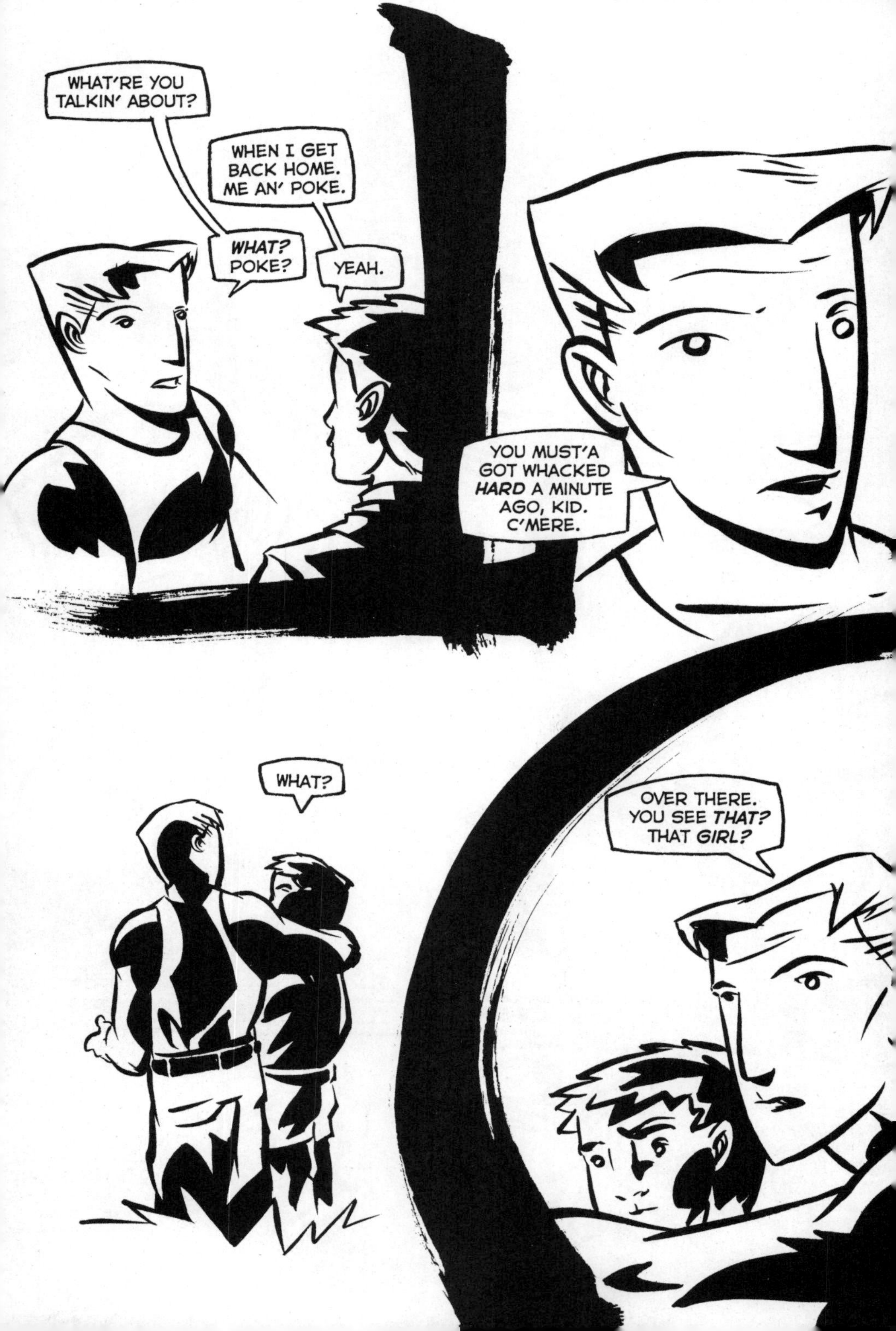
WHAT'RE YOU TALKIN' ABOUT?
WHEN I GET BACK HOME. ME AN' POKE.
WHAT? POKE?
YEAH.
YOU MUST'A GOT WHACKED HARD A MINUTE AGO, KID. C'MERE.
WHAT?
OVER THERE. YOU SEE THAT? THAT GIRL?

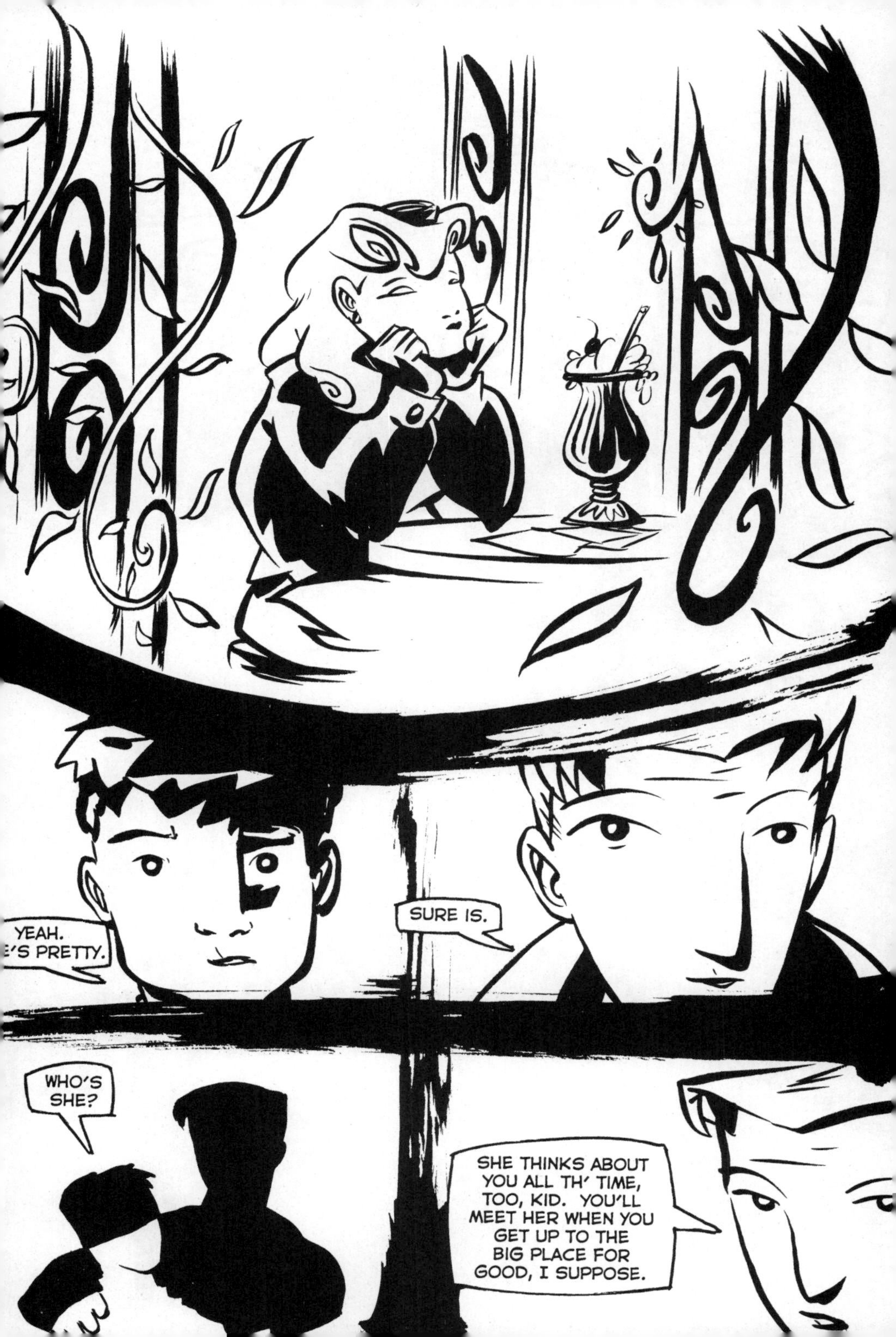
YEAH. 'S PRETTY.
SURE IS.
WHO'S SHE?
SHE THINKS ABOUT YOU ALL TH' TIME, TOO, KID. YOU'LL MEET HER WHEN YOU GET UP TO THE BIG PLACE FOR GOOD, I SUPPOSE.

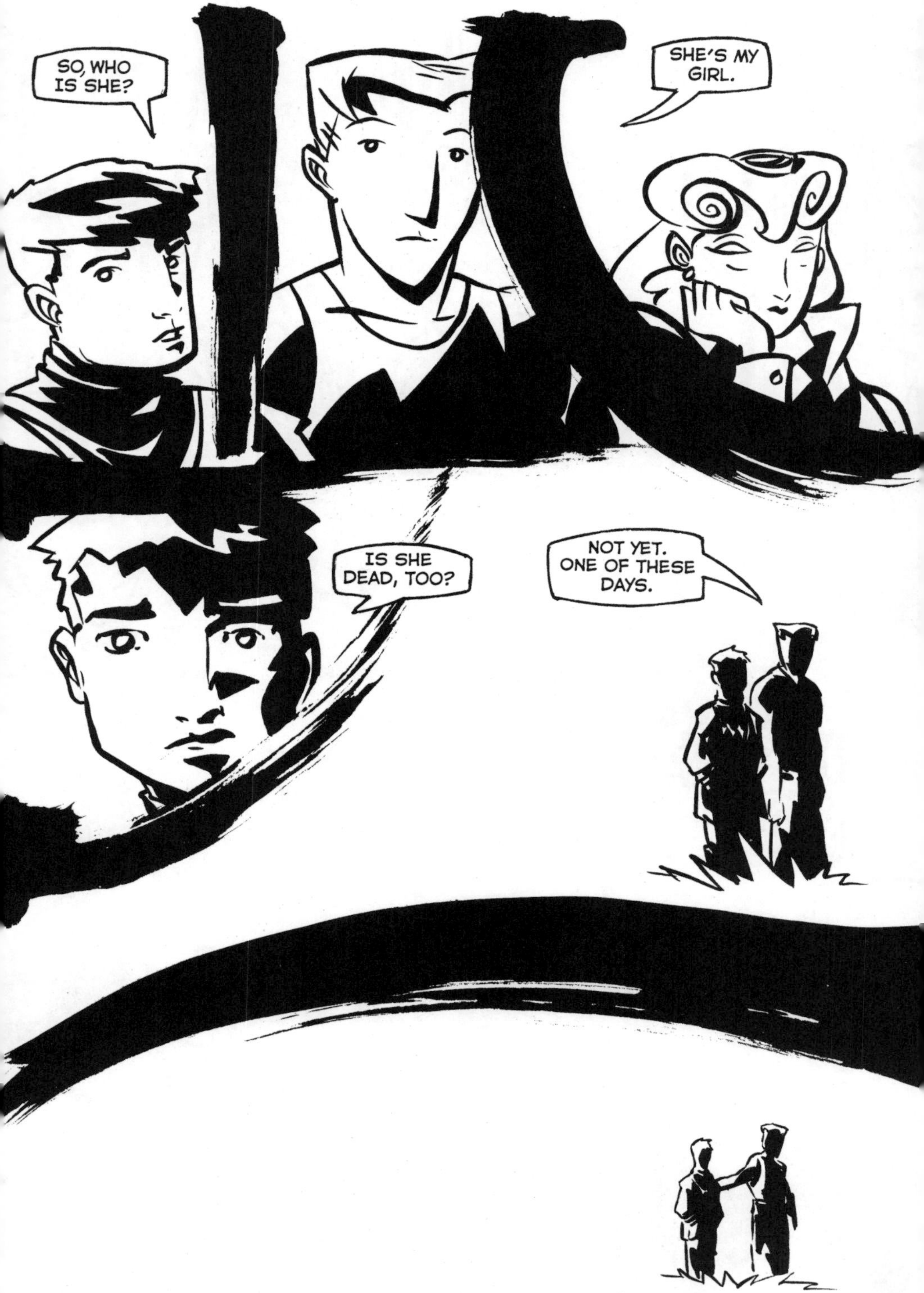
SO, WHO IS SHE?
SHE'S MY GIRL.
IS SHE DEAD, TOO?
NOT YET. ONE OF THESE DAYS.

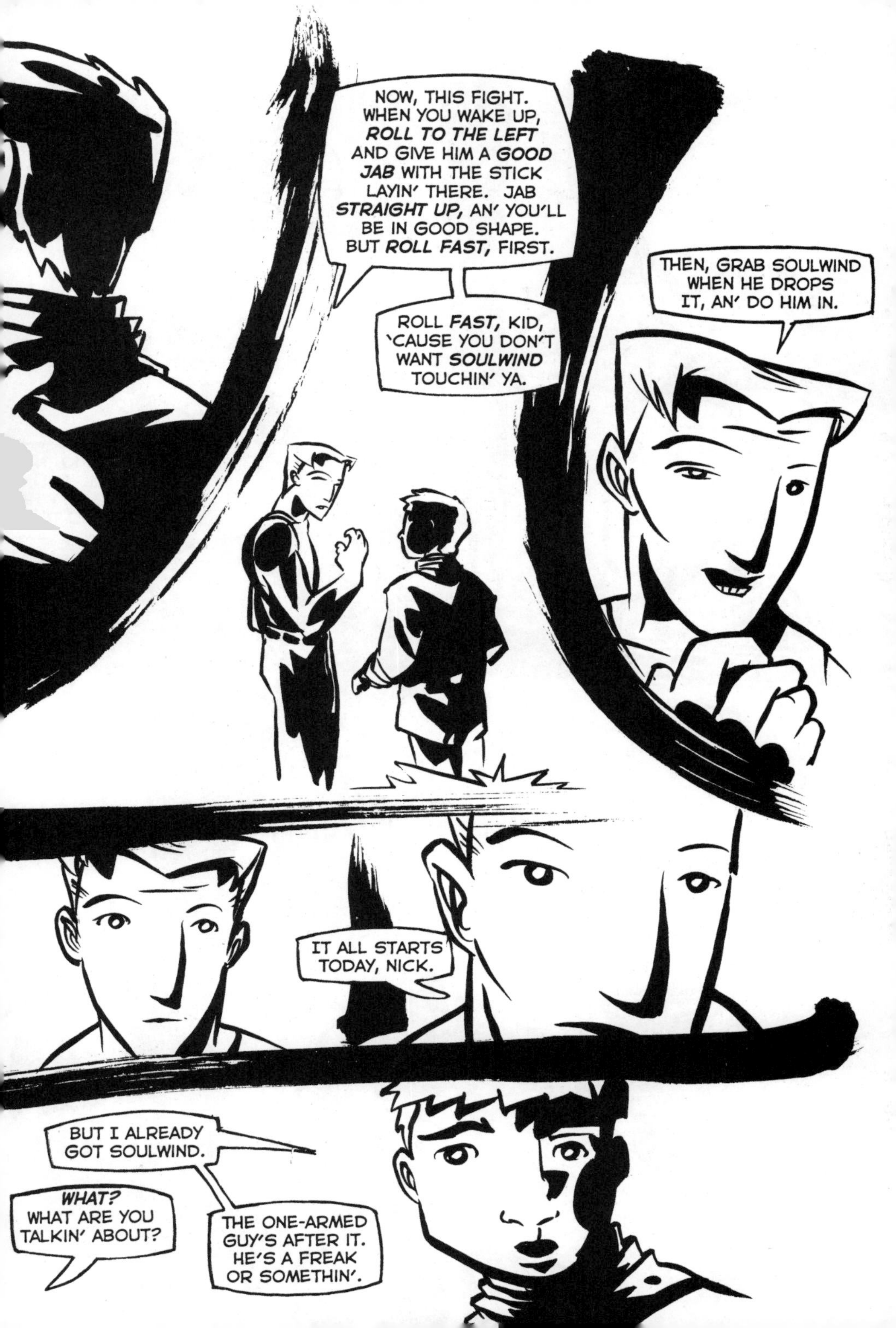
NOW, THIS FIGHT. WHEN YOU WAKE UP, ROLL TO THE LEFT AND GIVE HIM A GOOD JAB WITH THE STICK LAYIN' THERE. JAB STRAIGHT UP, AN' YOU'LL BE IN GOOD SHAPE. BUT ROLL FAST, FIRST.
ROLL FAST, KID, 'CAUSE YOU DON'T WANT SOULWIND TOUCHIN' YA.
THEN, GRAB SOULWIND WHEN HE DROPS IT, AN' DO HIM IN.
IT ALL STARTS TODAY, NICK.
BUT I ALREADY GOT SOULWIND.
WHAT? WHAT ARE YOU TALKIN' ABOUT?
THE ONE-ARMED GUY'S AFTER IT. HE'S A FREAK OR SOMETHIN'.

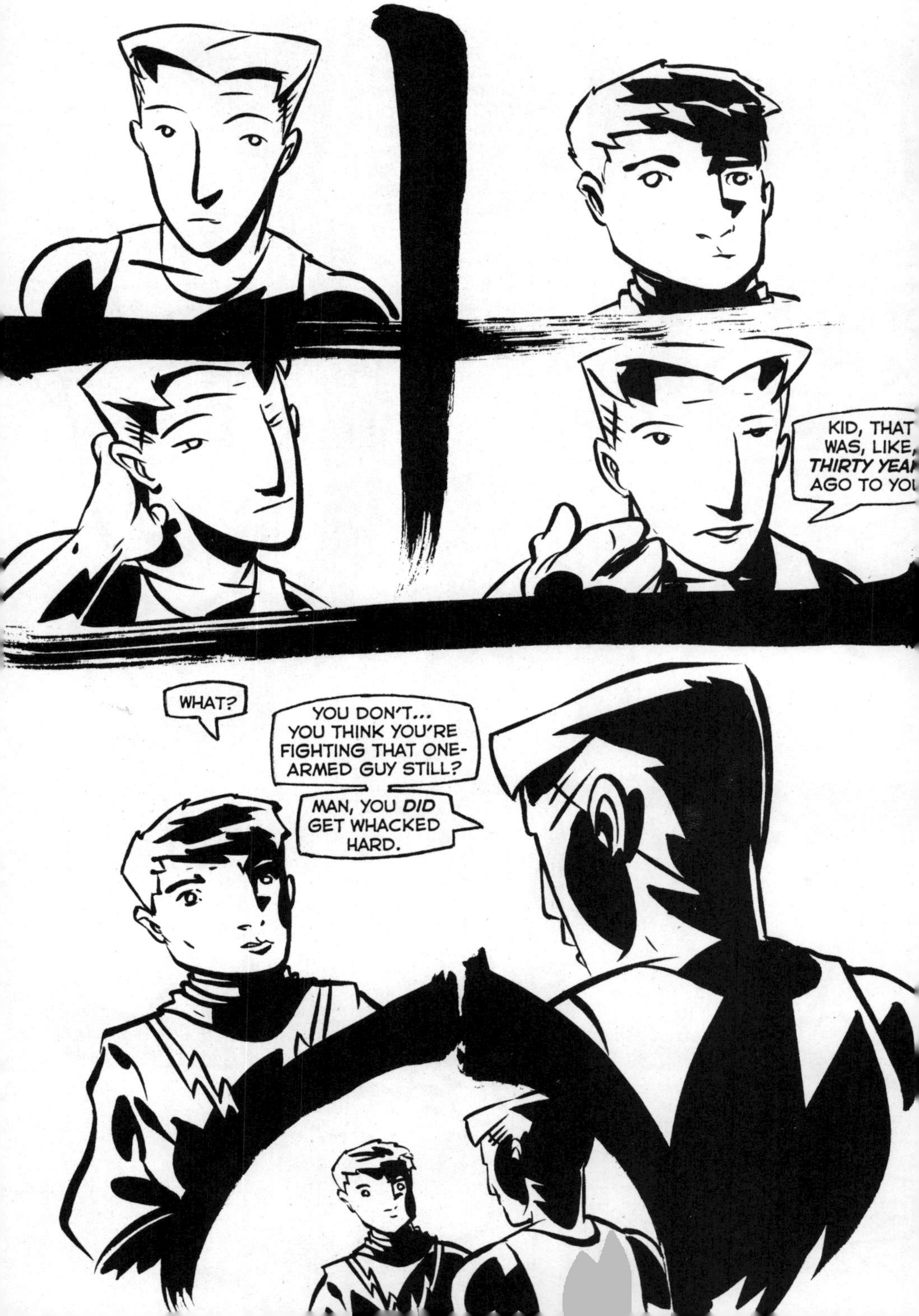

KID, THAT WAS, LIKE, THIRTY YEA AGO TO YO
WHAT?
YOU DON'T... YOU THINK YOU'RE FIGHTING THAT ONE-ARMED GUY STILL?
MAN, YOU *DID* GET WHACKED HARD.

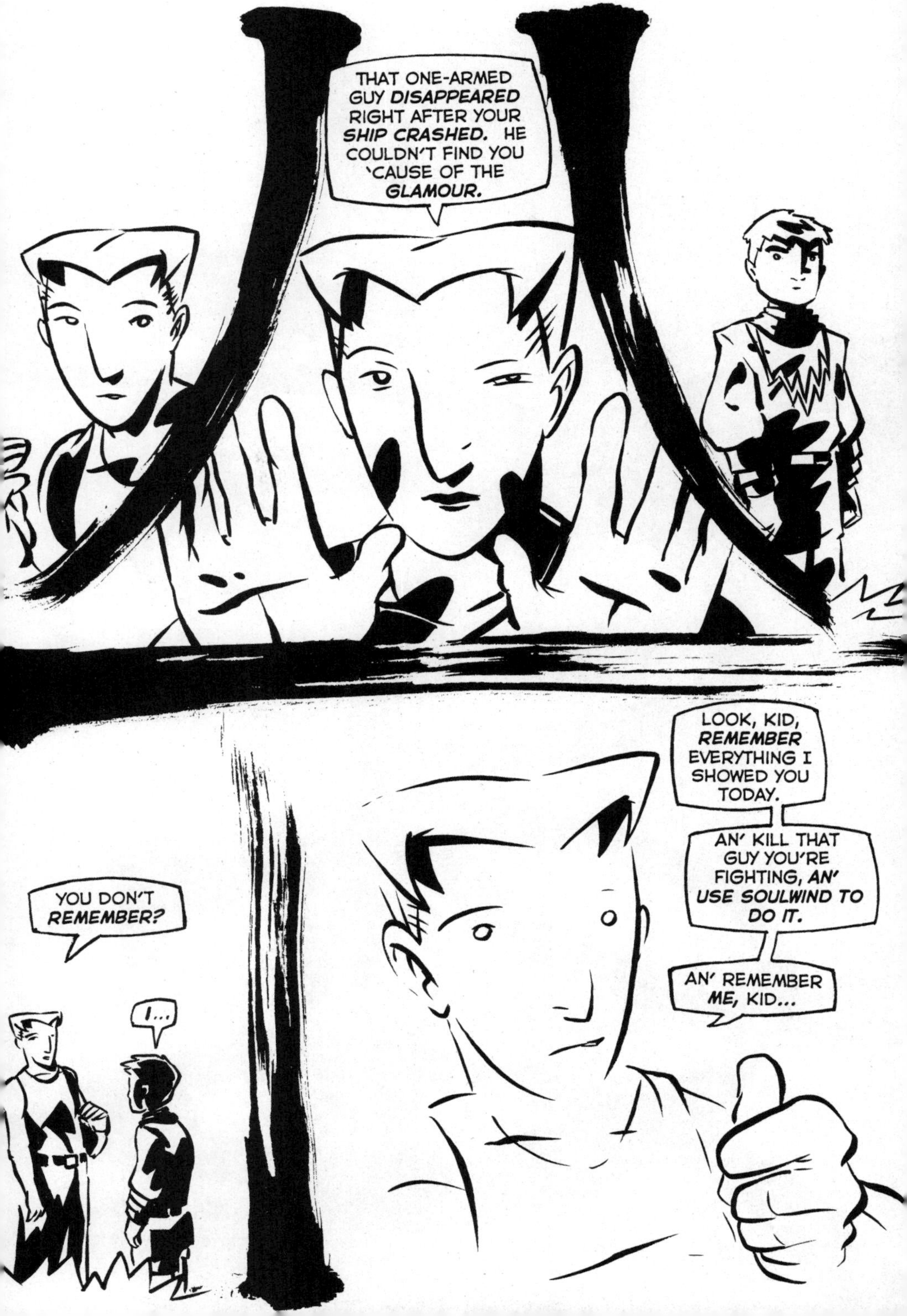
THAT ONE-ARMED GUY DISAPPEARED RIGHT AFTER YOUR SHIP CRASHED. HE COULDN'T FIND YOU 'CAUSE OF THE GLAMOUR.
YOU DON'T REMEMBER?
I...
LOOK, KID, REMEMBER EVERYTHING I SHOWED YOU TODAY.
AN' KILL THAT GUY YOU'RE FIGHTING, AN' USE SOULWIND TO DO IT.
AN' REMEMBER ME, KID...

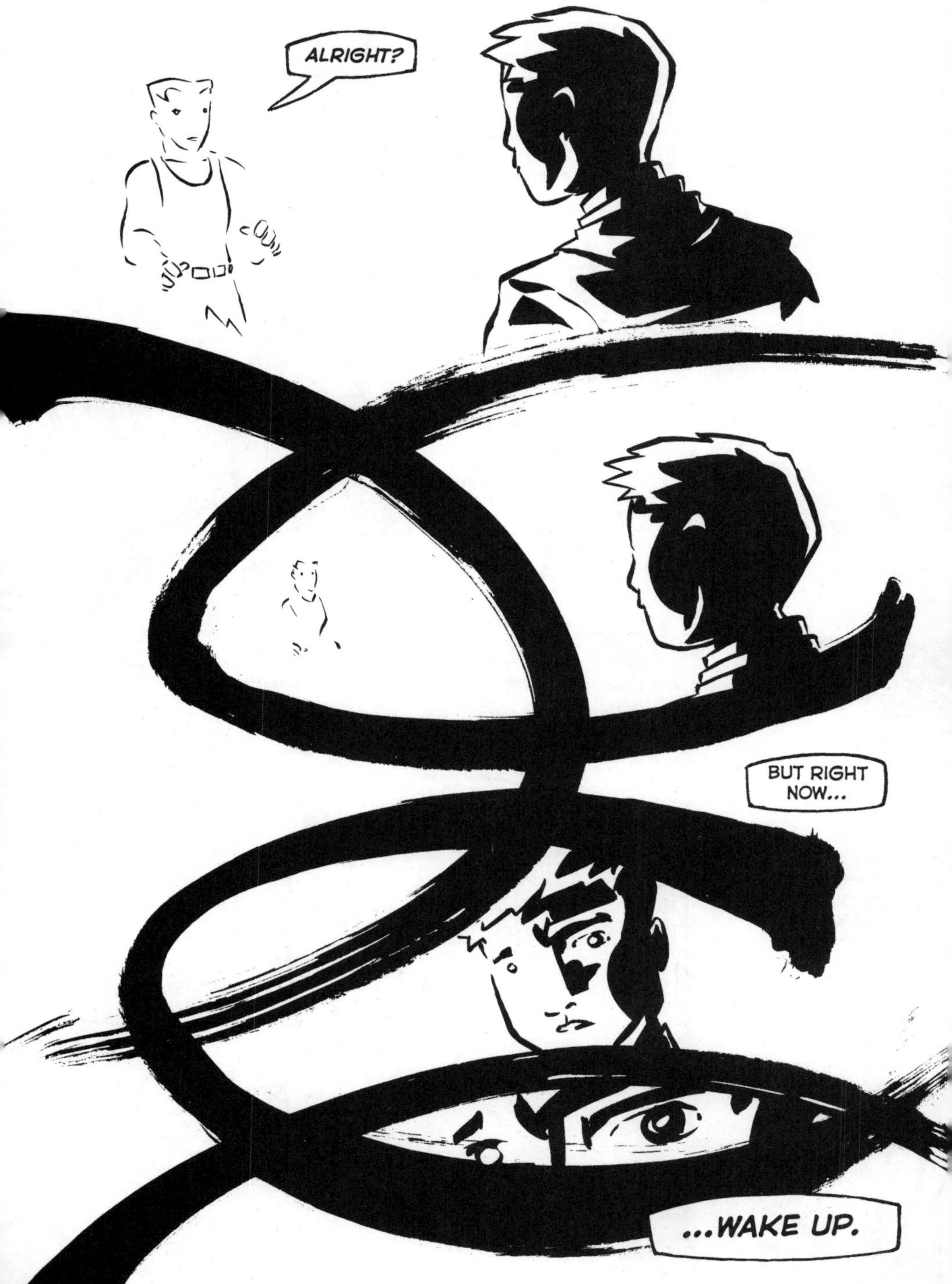
ALRIGHT?
BUT RIGHT NOW...
...WAKE UP.

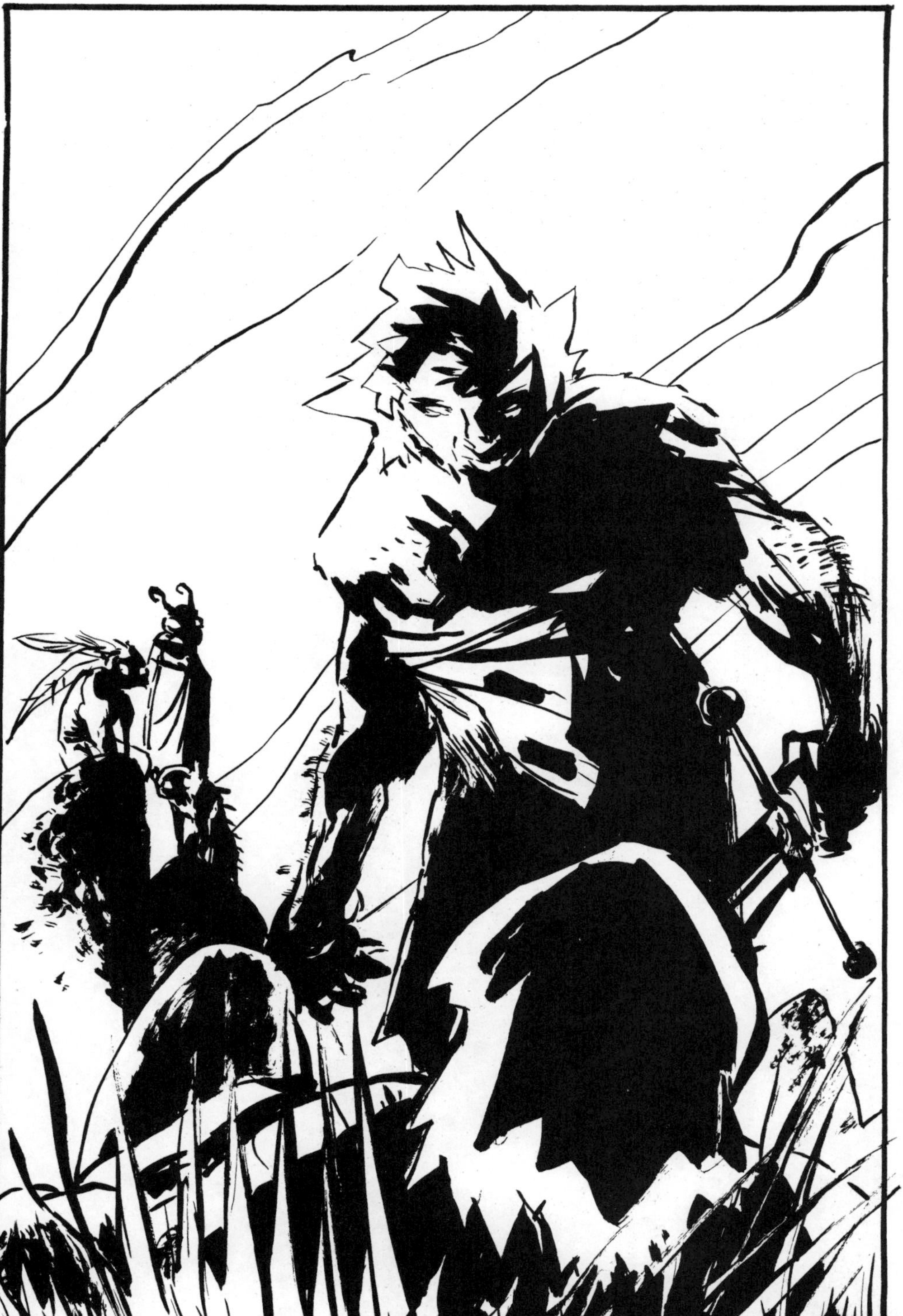

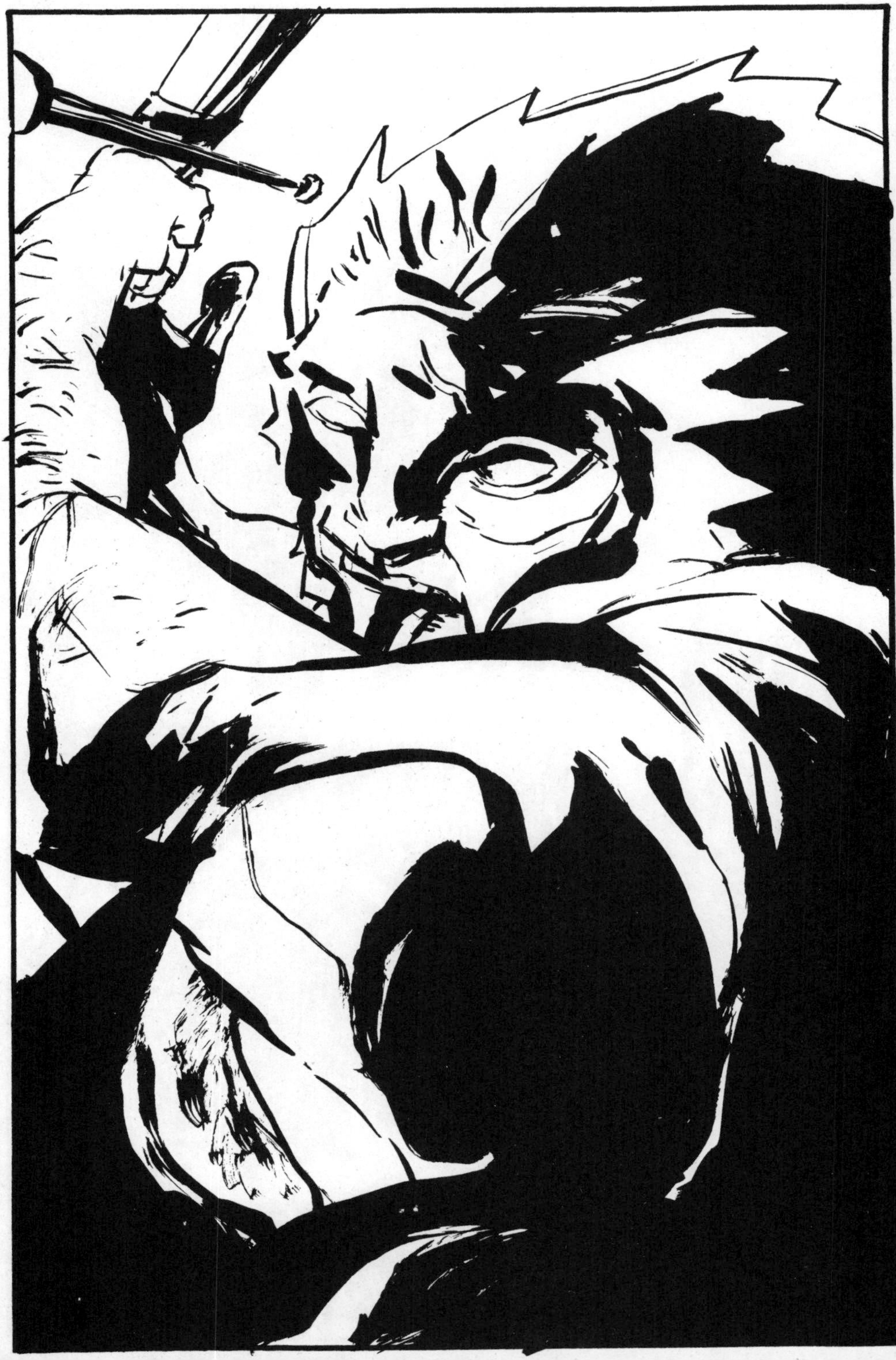

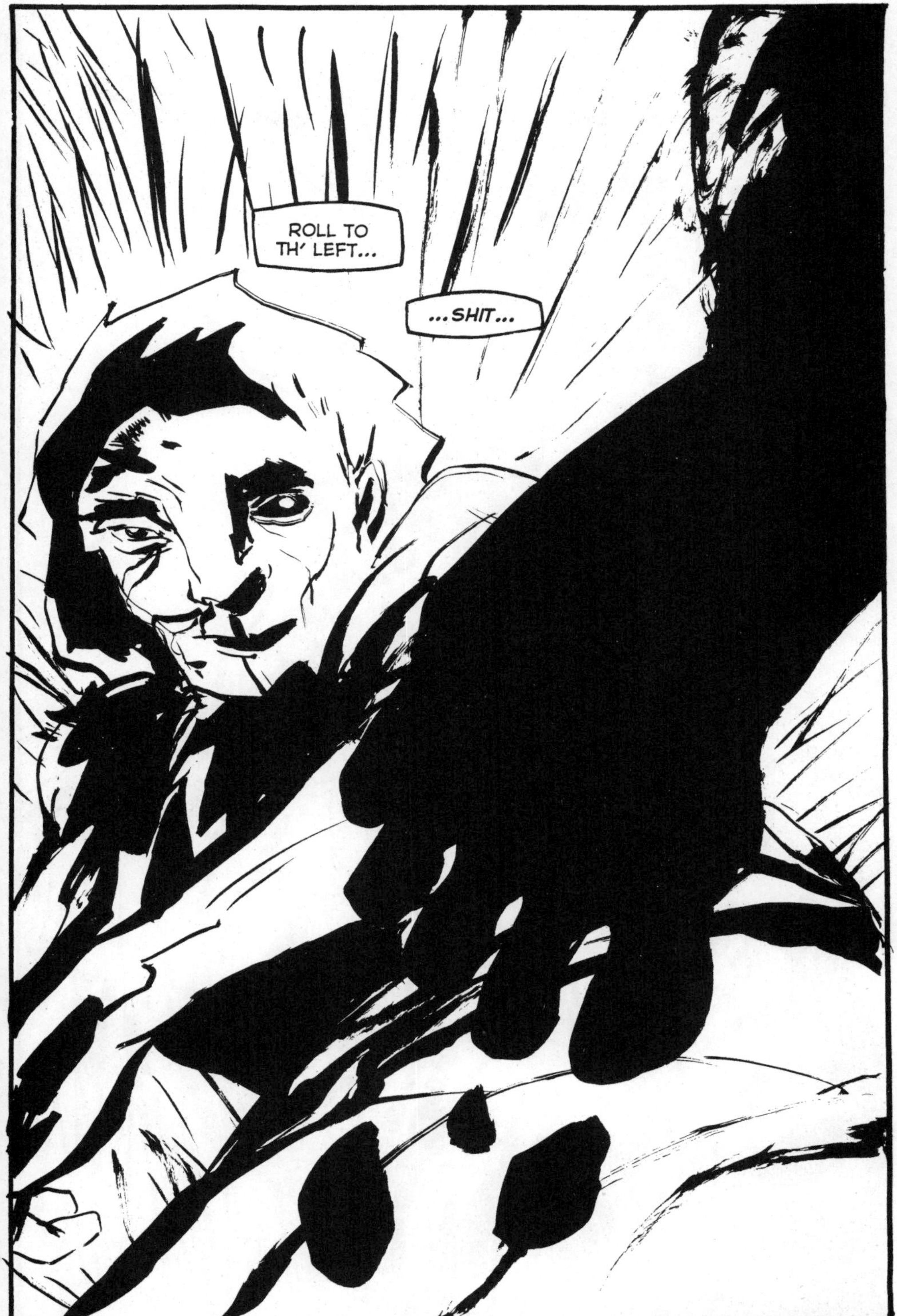
ROLL TO TH' LEFT...
...SHIT...

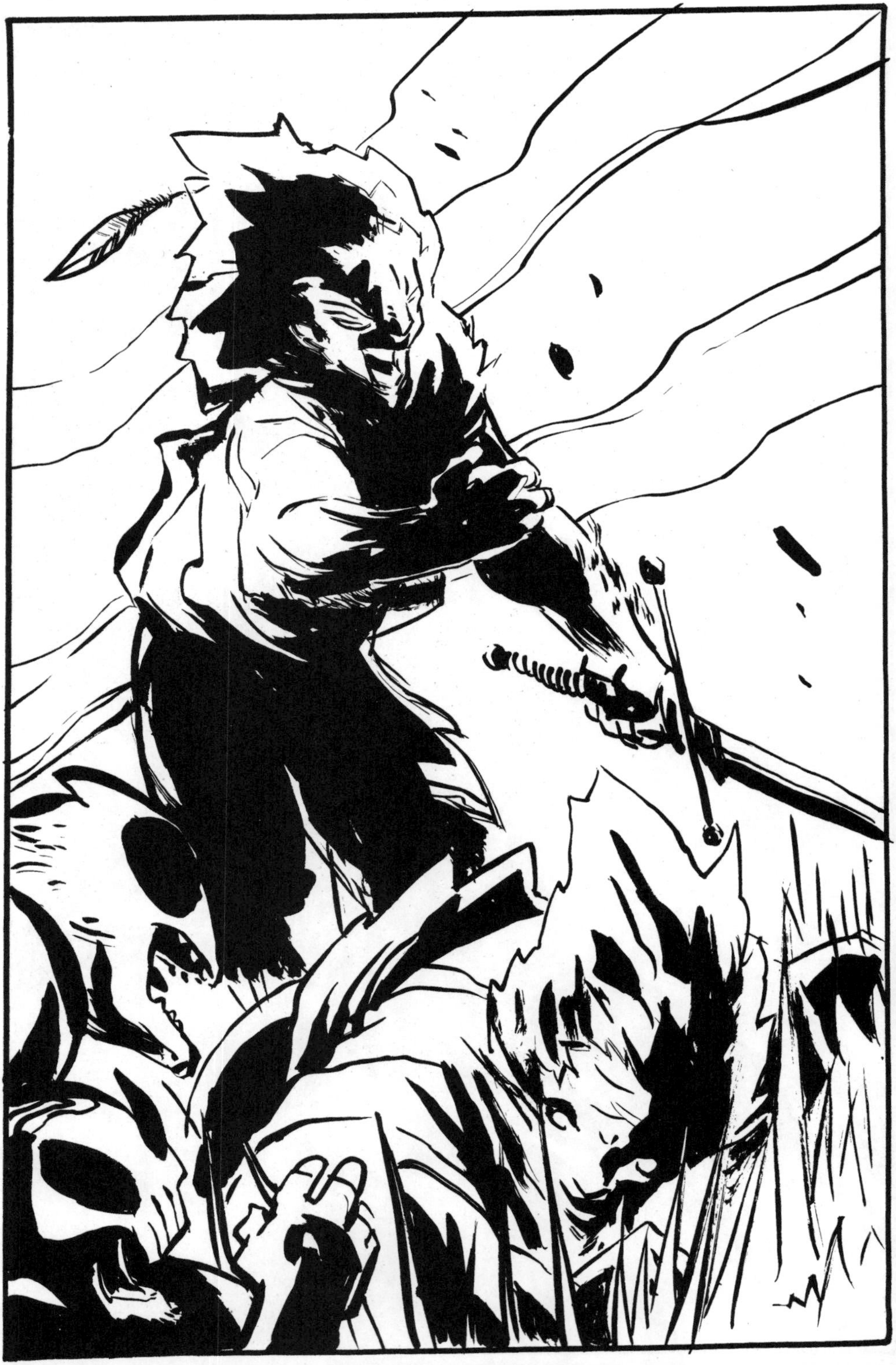

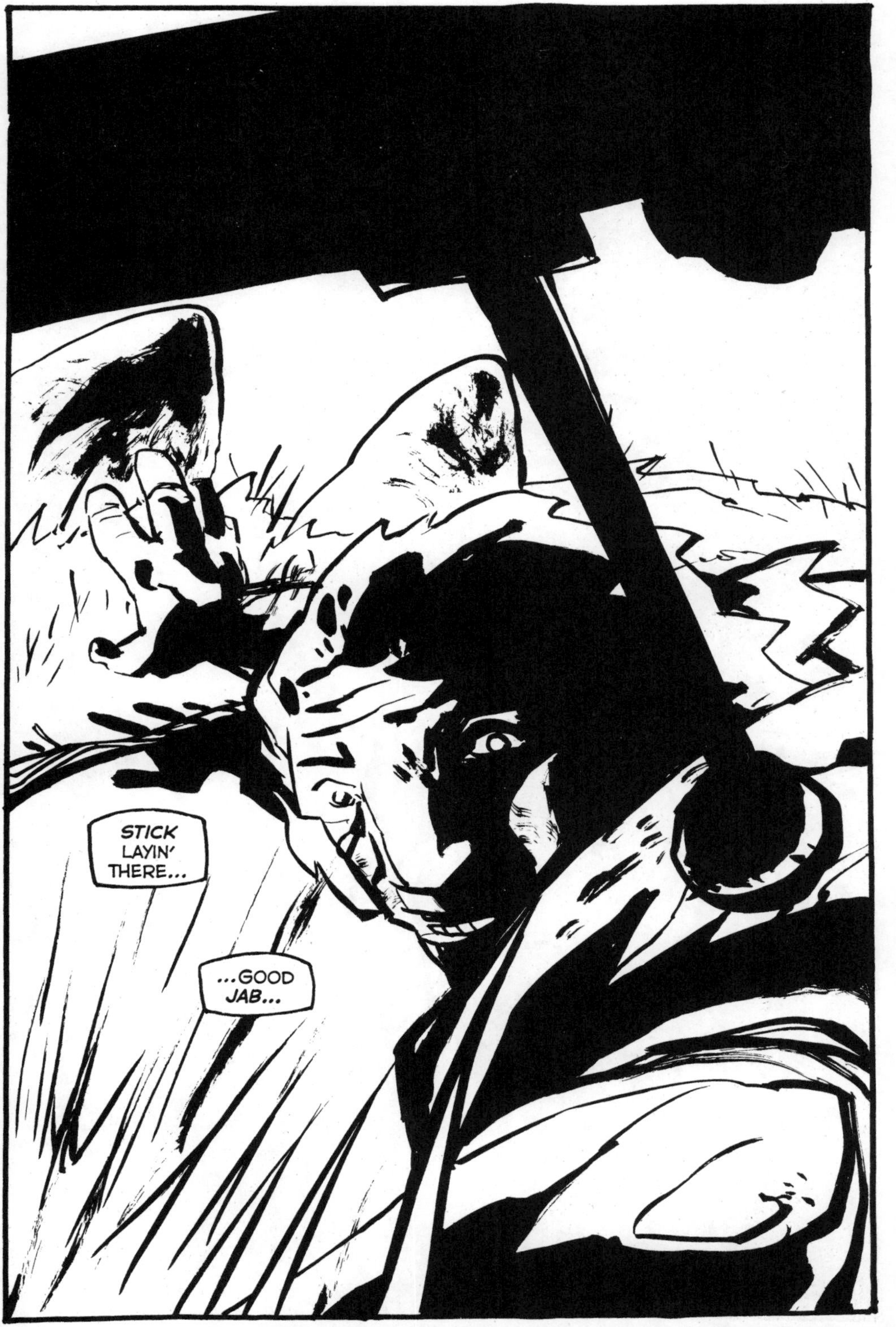
STICK LAYIN' THERE...
...GOOD JAB...

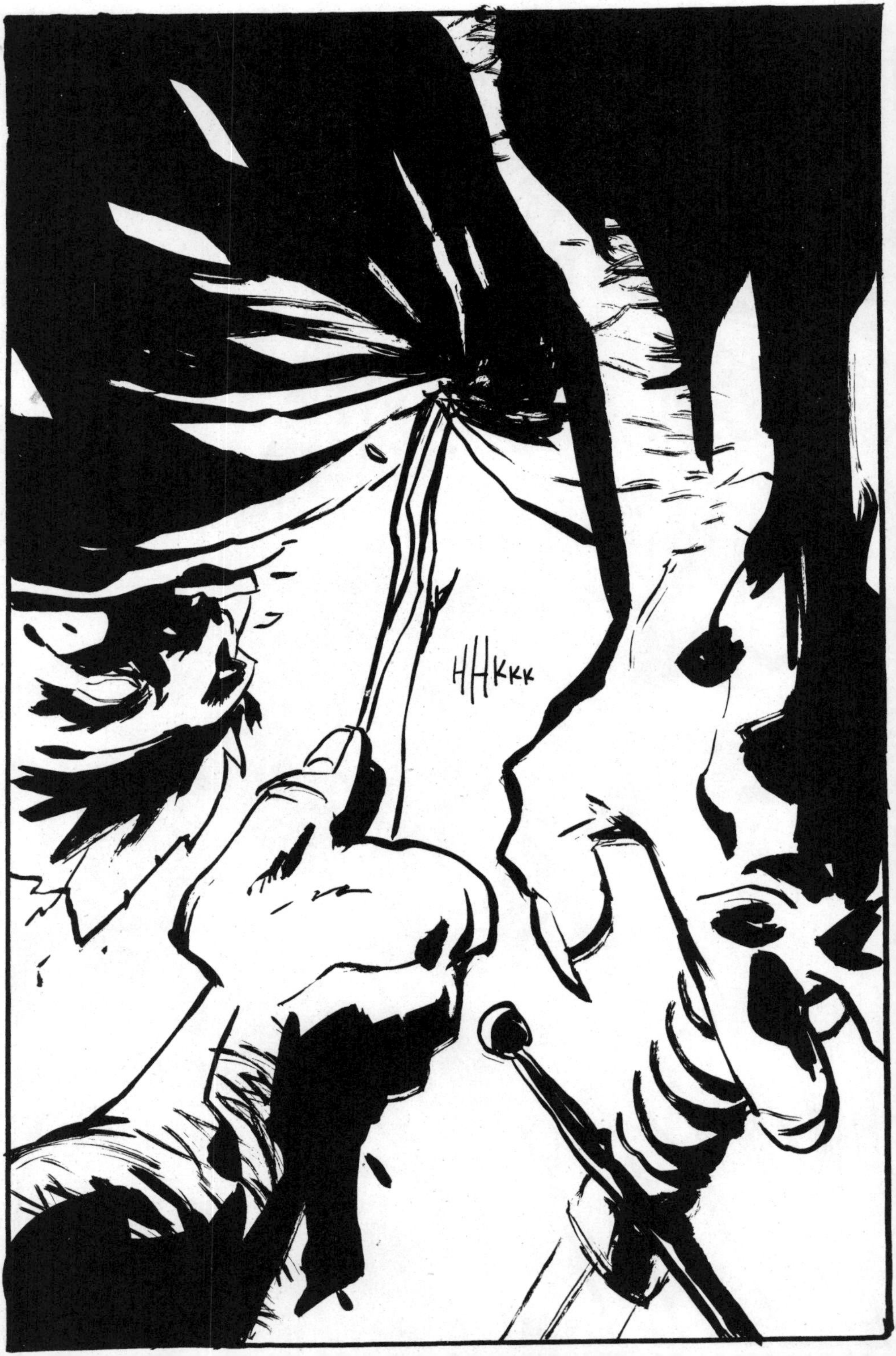
HHKKK

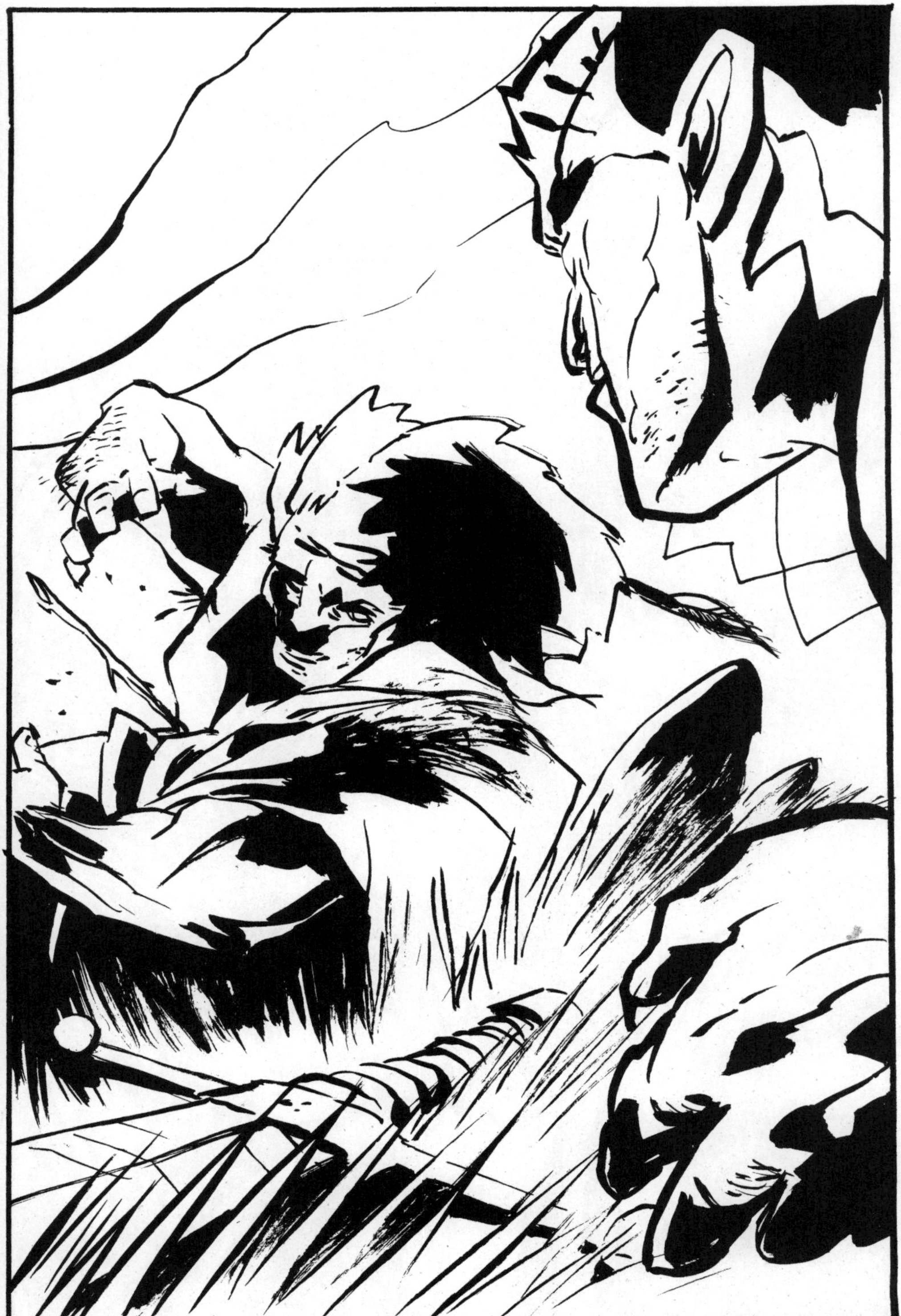

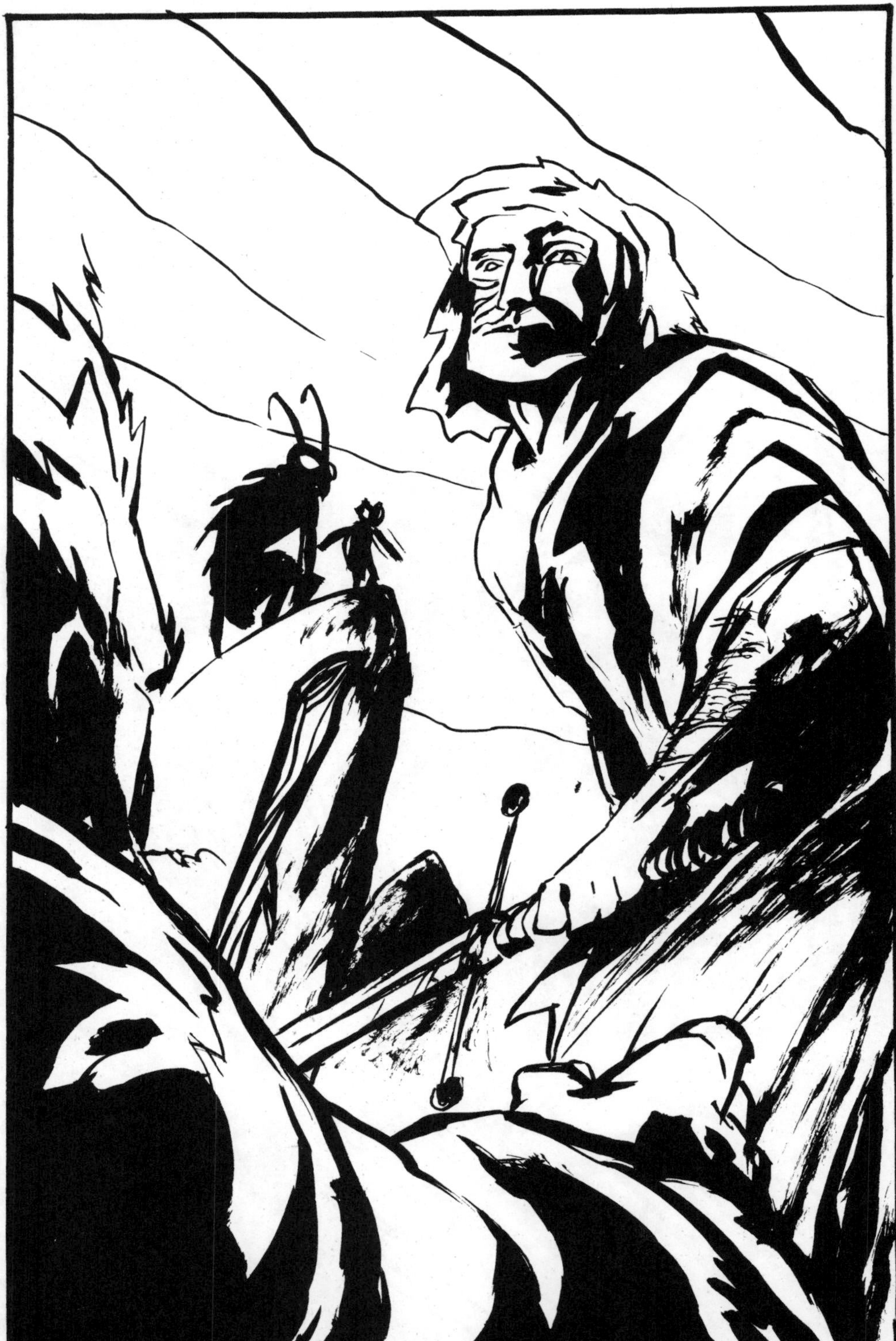

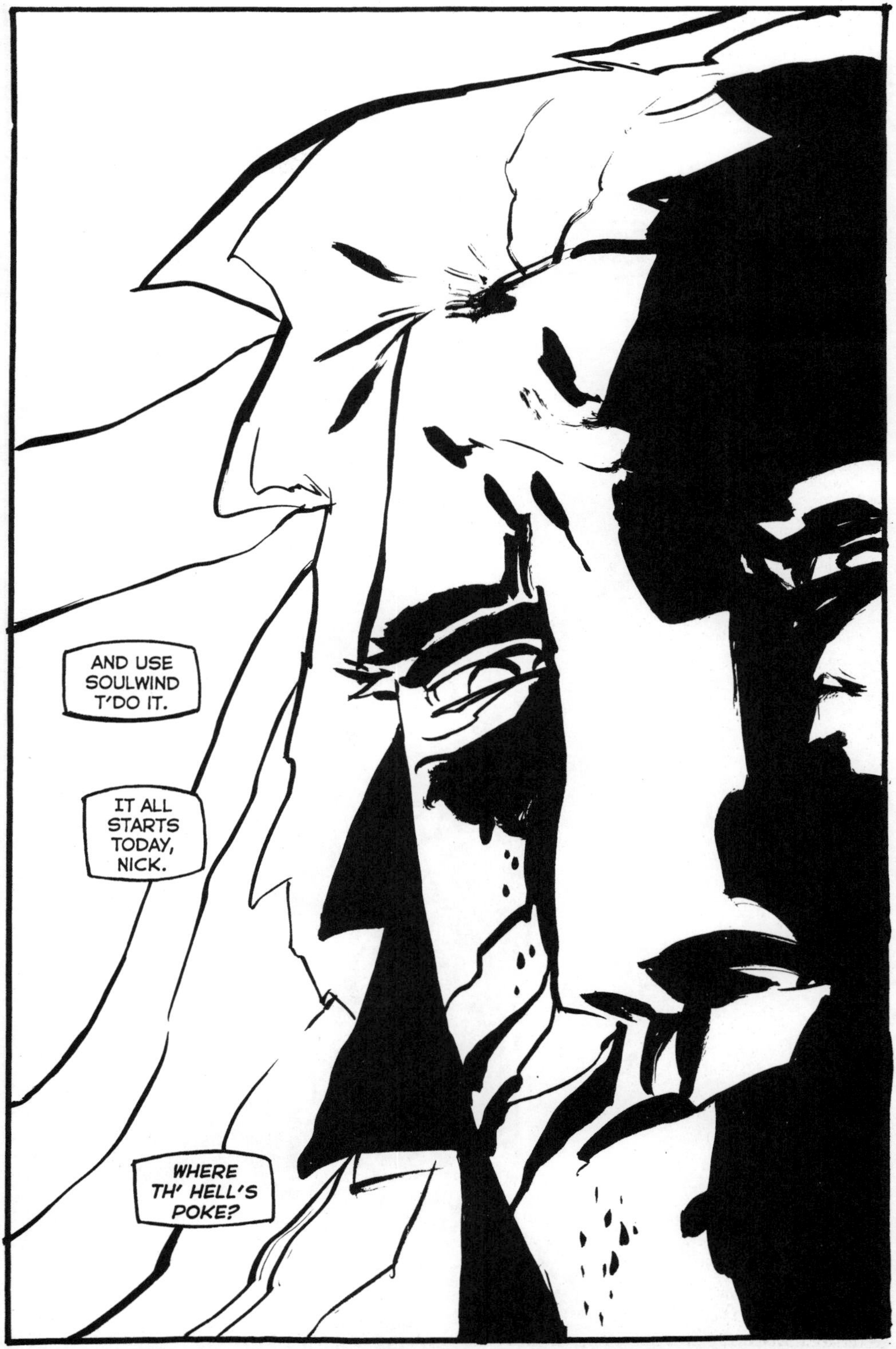
AND USE SOULWIND T'DO IT.
IT ALL STARTS TODAY, NICK.
WHERE TH' HELL'S POKE?

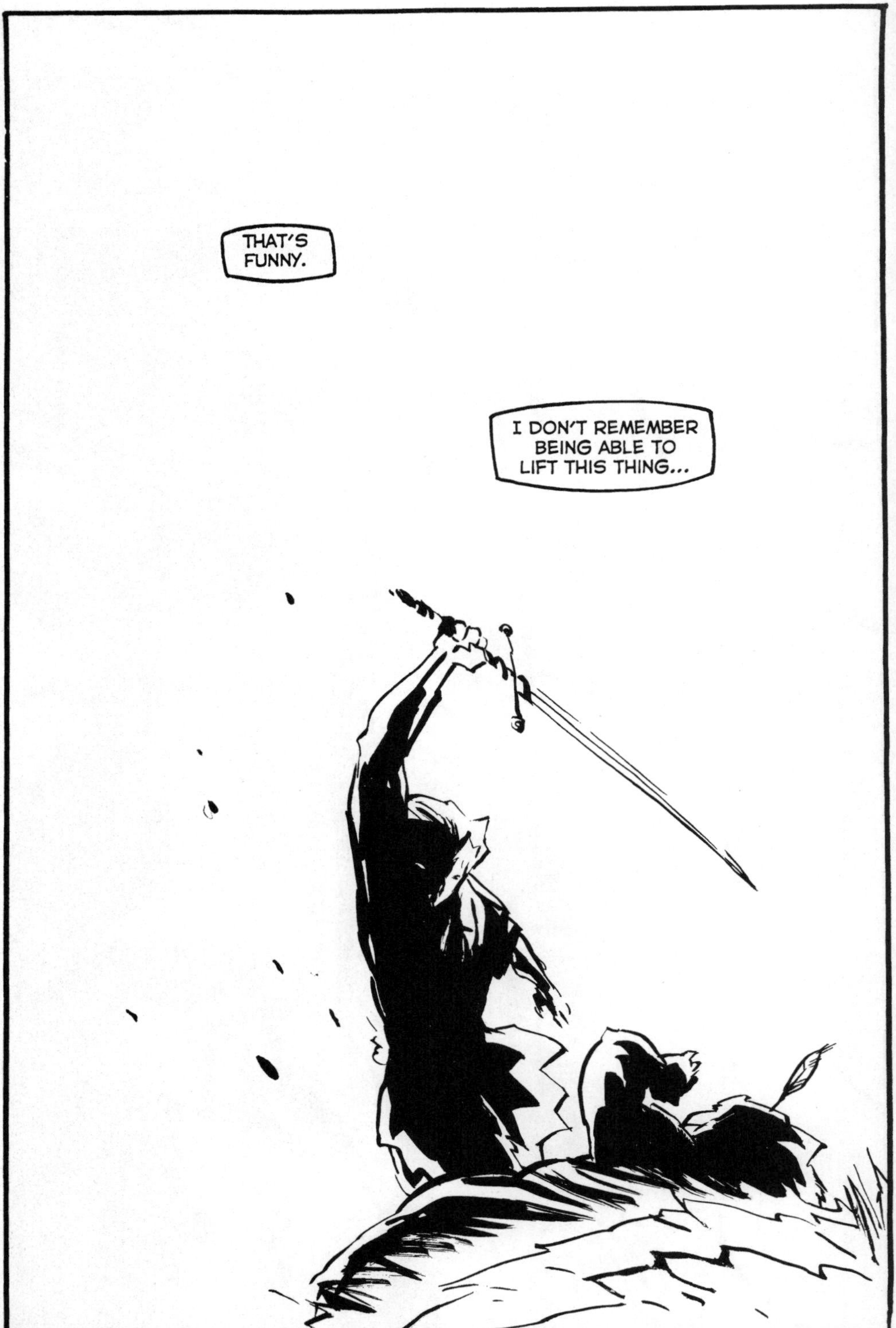
THAT'S FUNNY.
I DON'T REMEMBER BEING ABLE TO LIFT THIS THING...

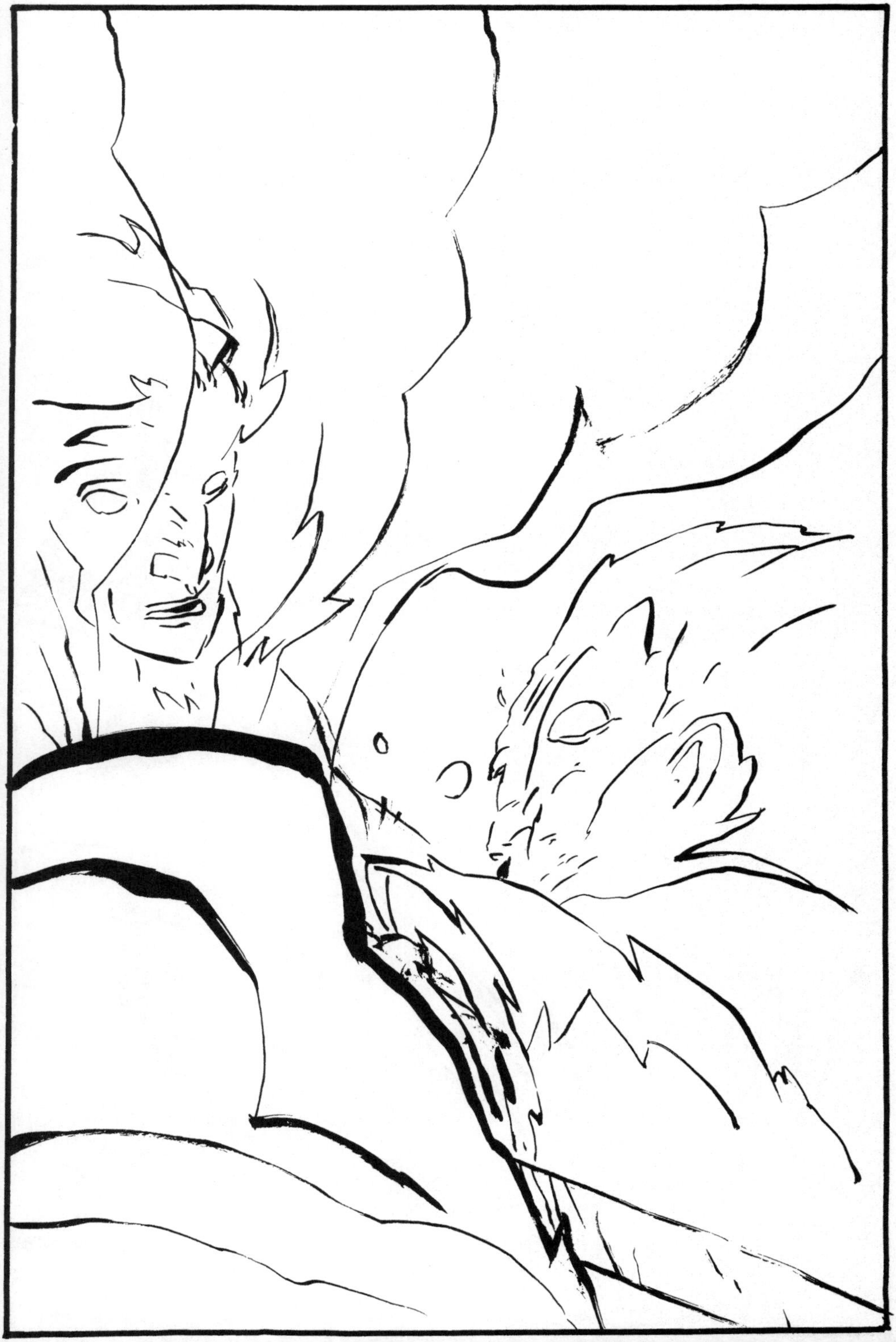

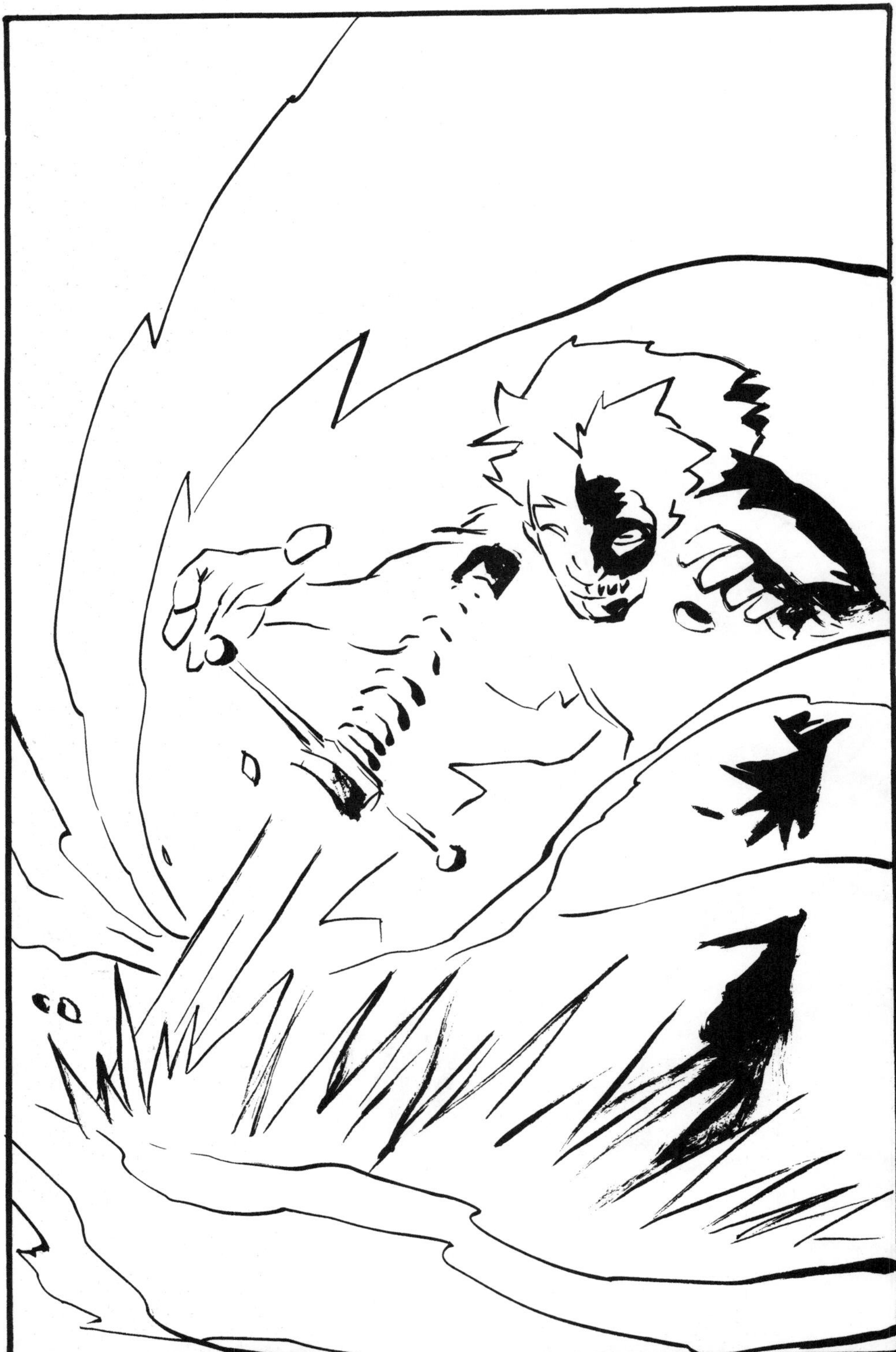

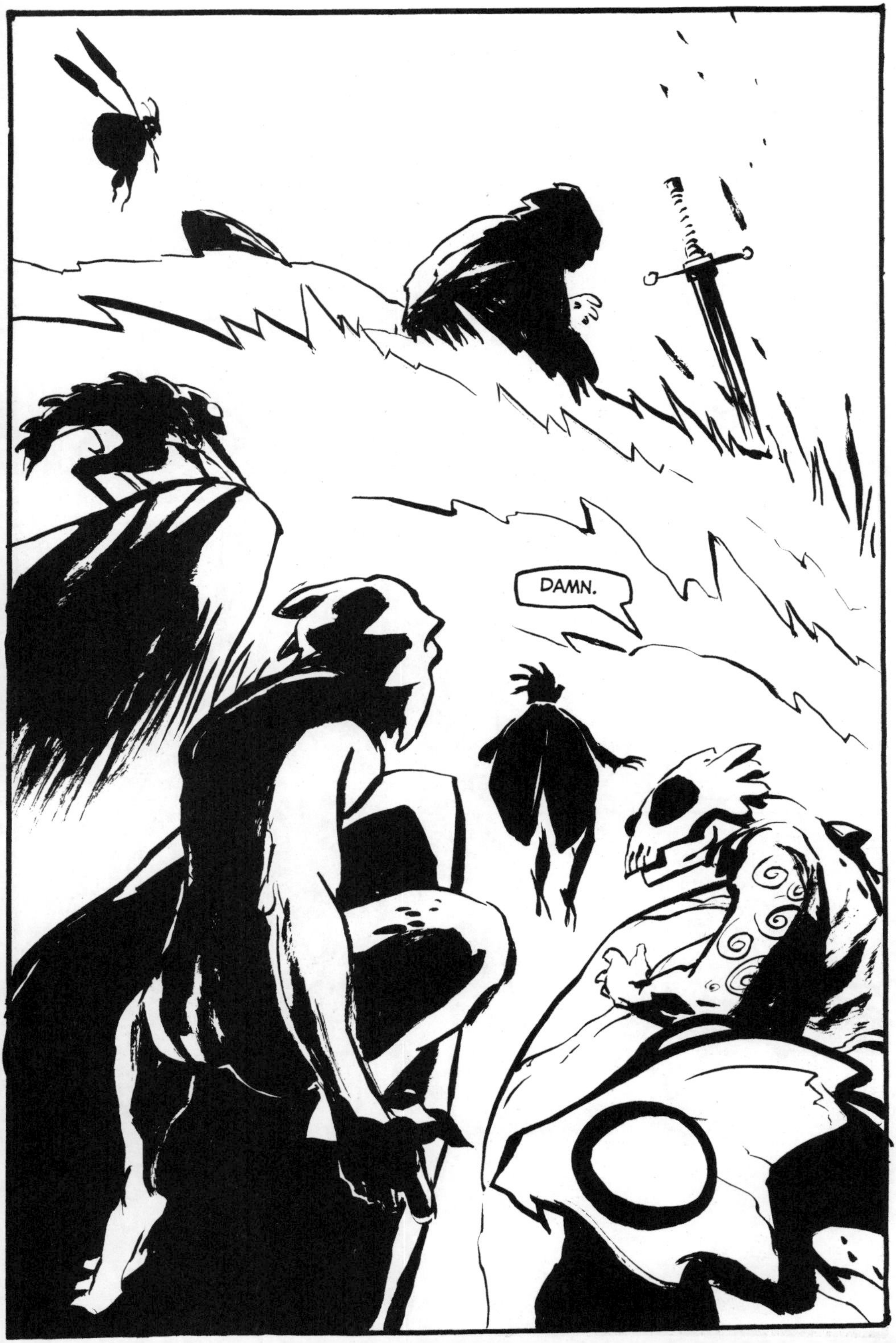
DAMN.

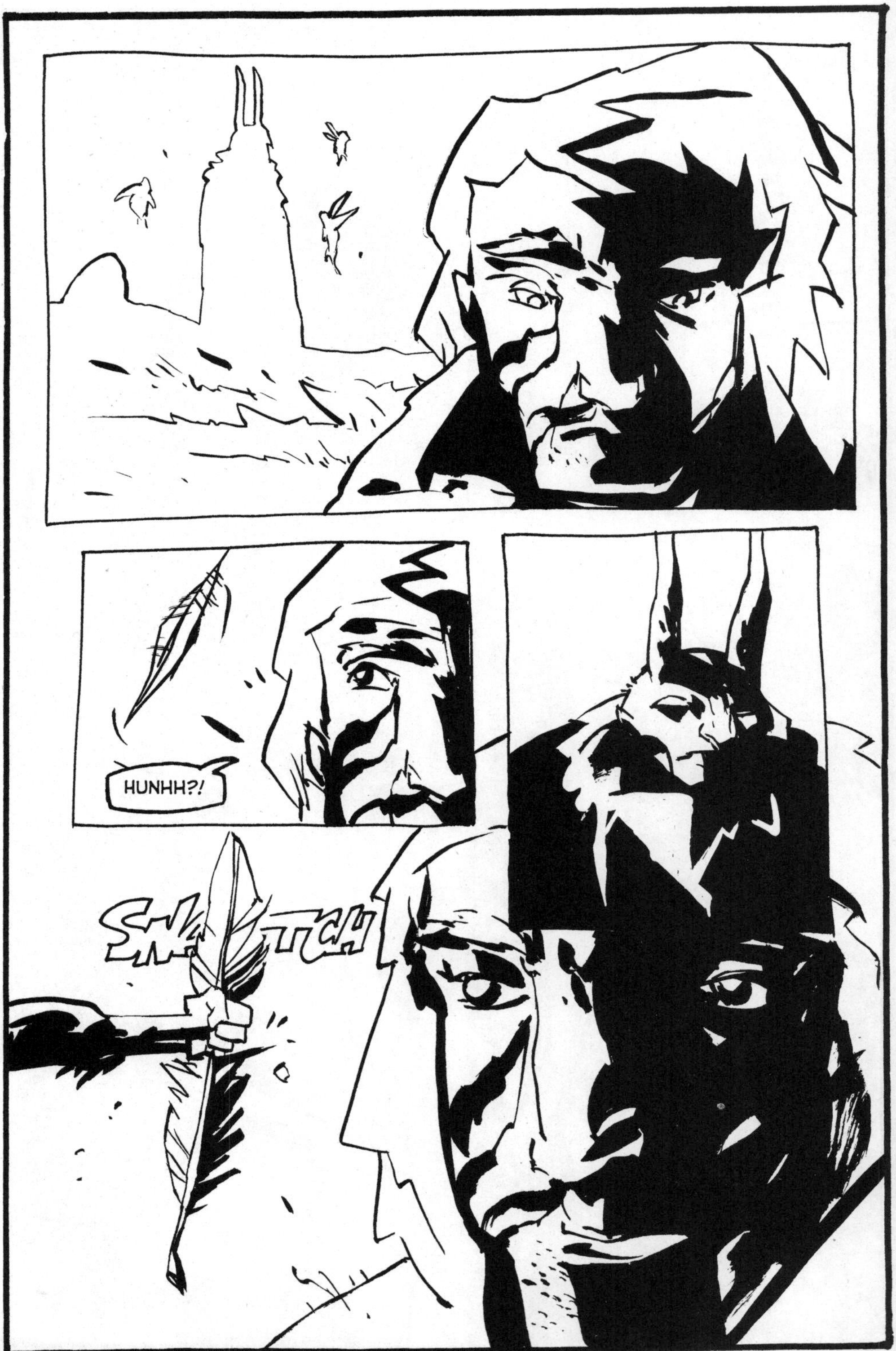
HUNHH?!
SNATCH

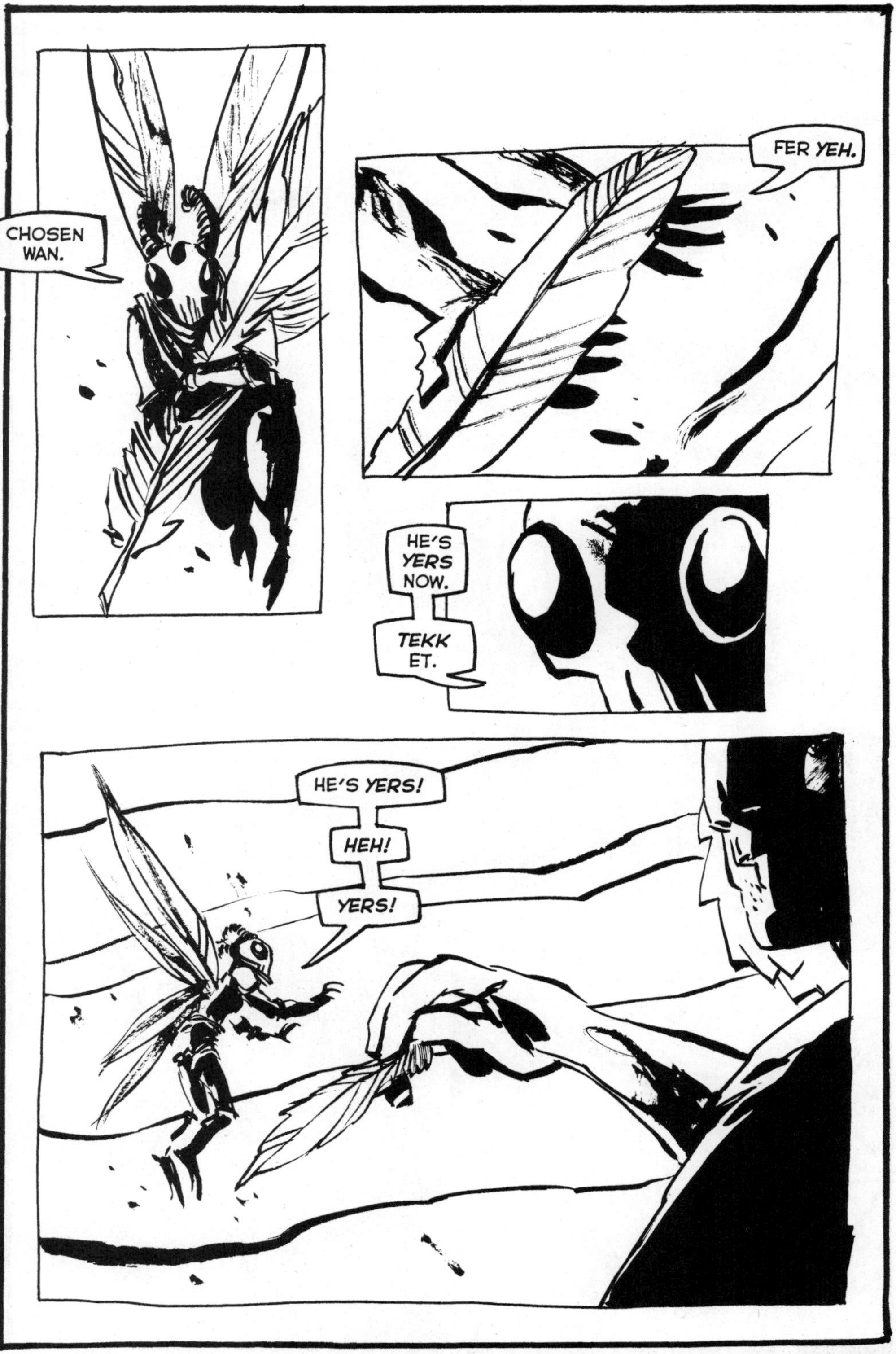
CHOSEN WAN.
FER YEH.
HE'S YERS NOW.
TEKK ET.
HE'S YERS!
HEH!
YERS!

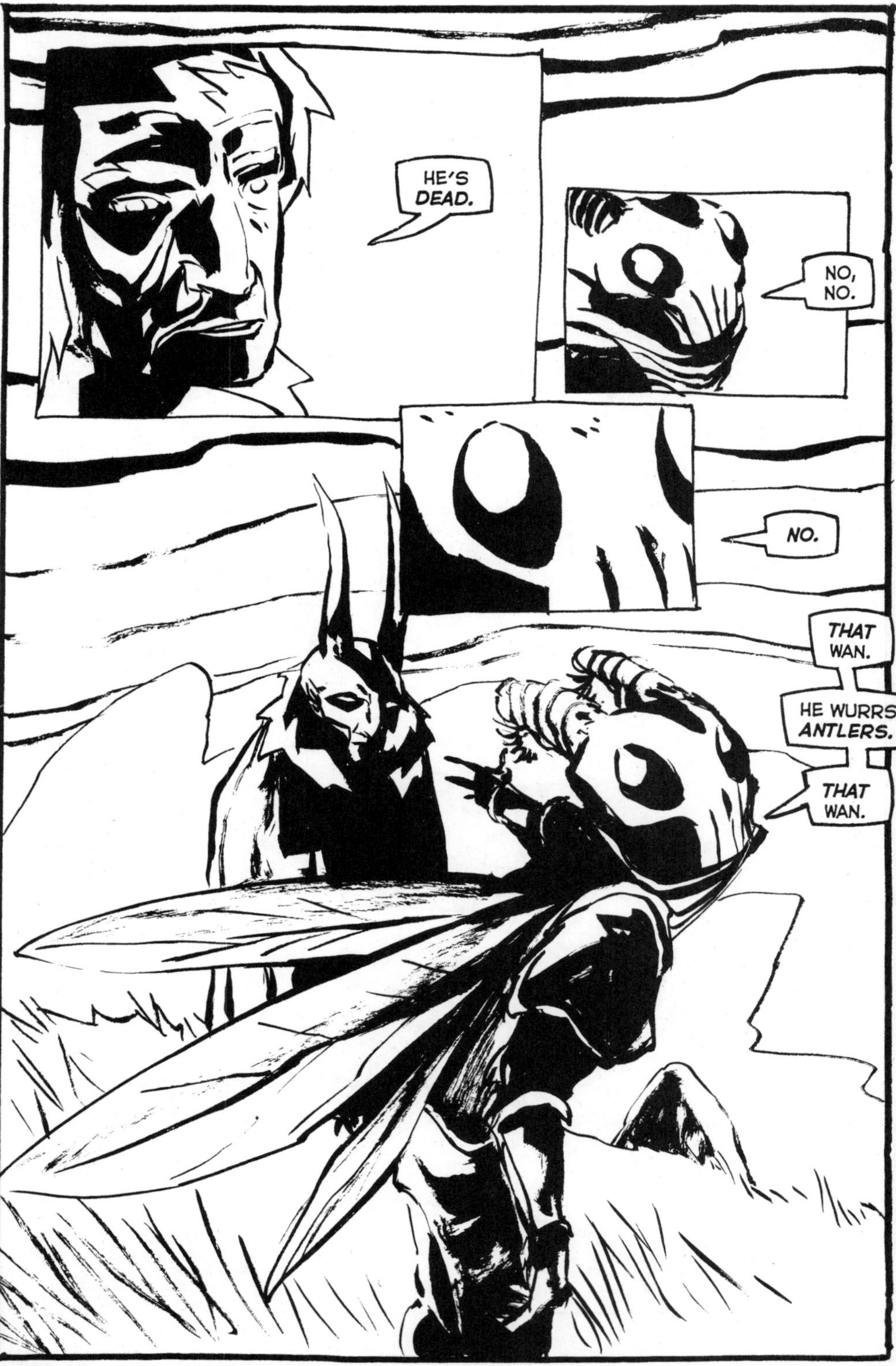
HE'S DEAD.
NO, NO.
NO.
THAT WAN.
HE WURRS ANTLERS.
THAT WAN.

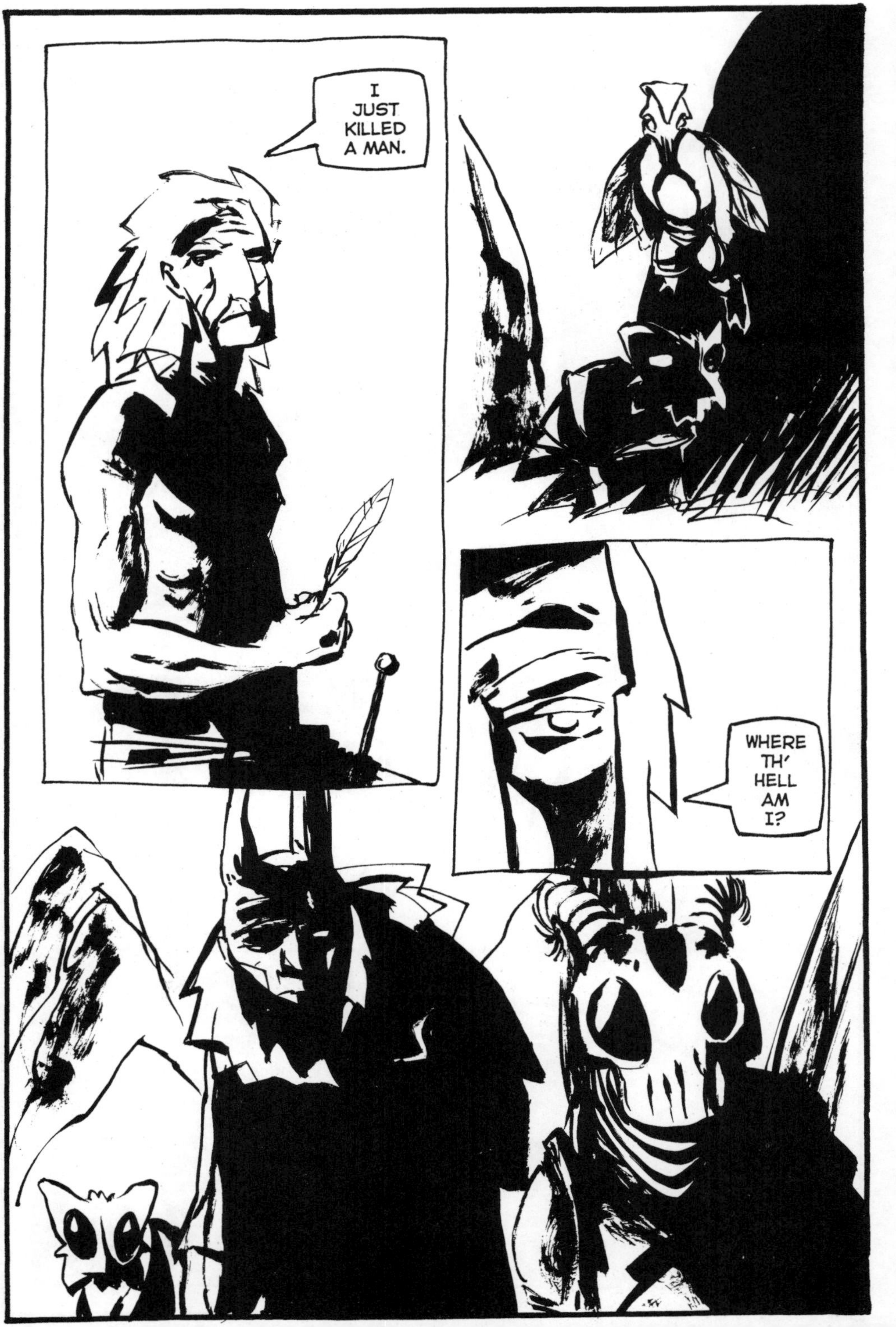
I JUST KILLED A MAN.
WHERE TH' HELL AM I?

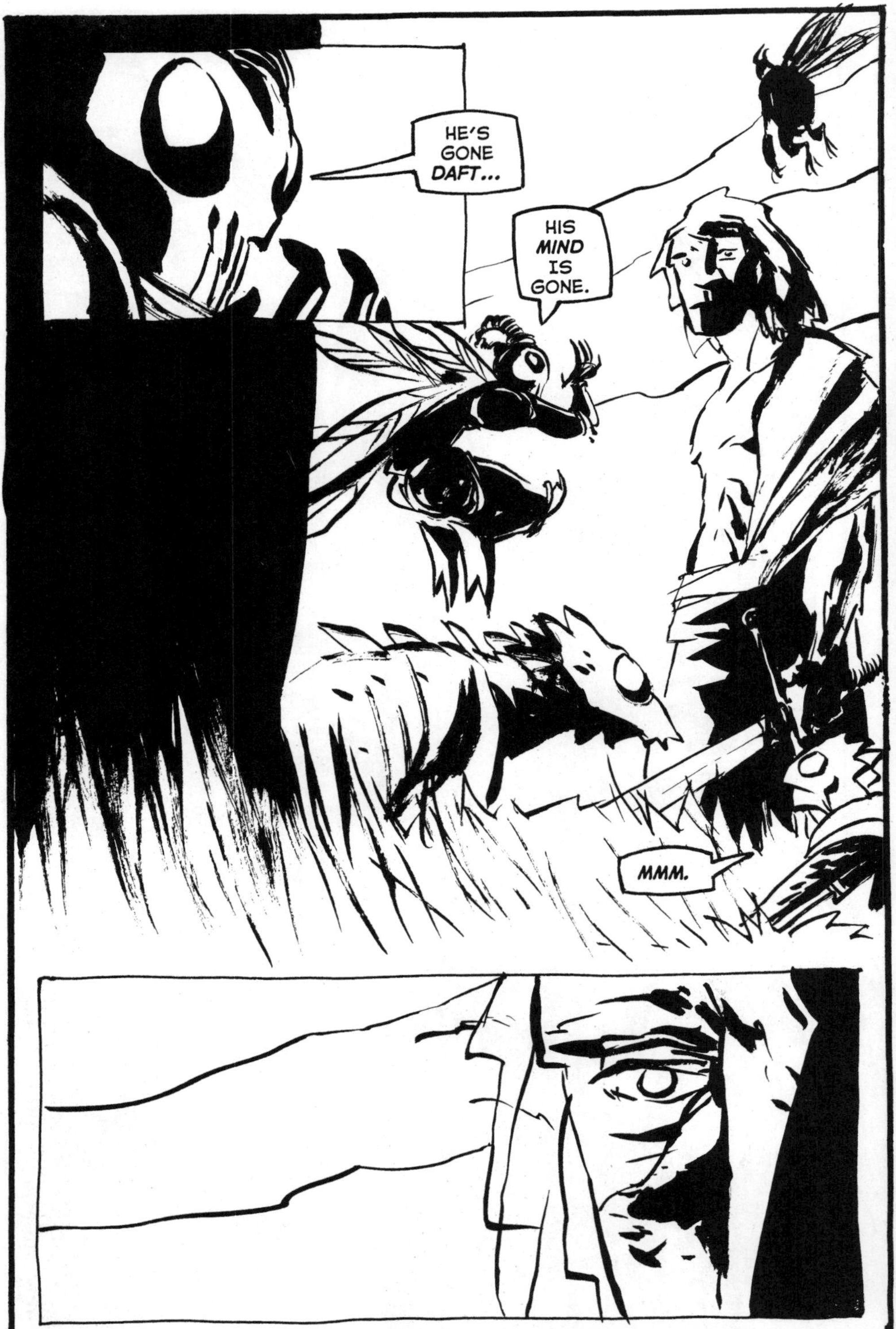
HE'S GONE DAFT...
HIS MIND IS GONE.
MMM.

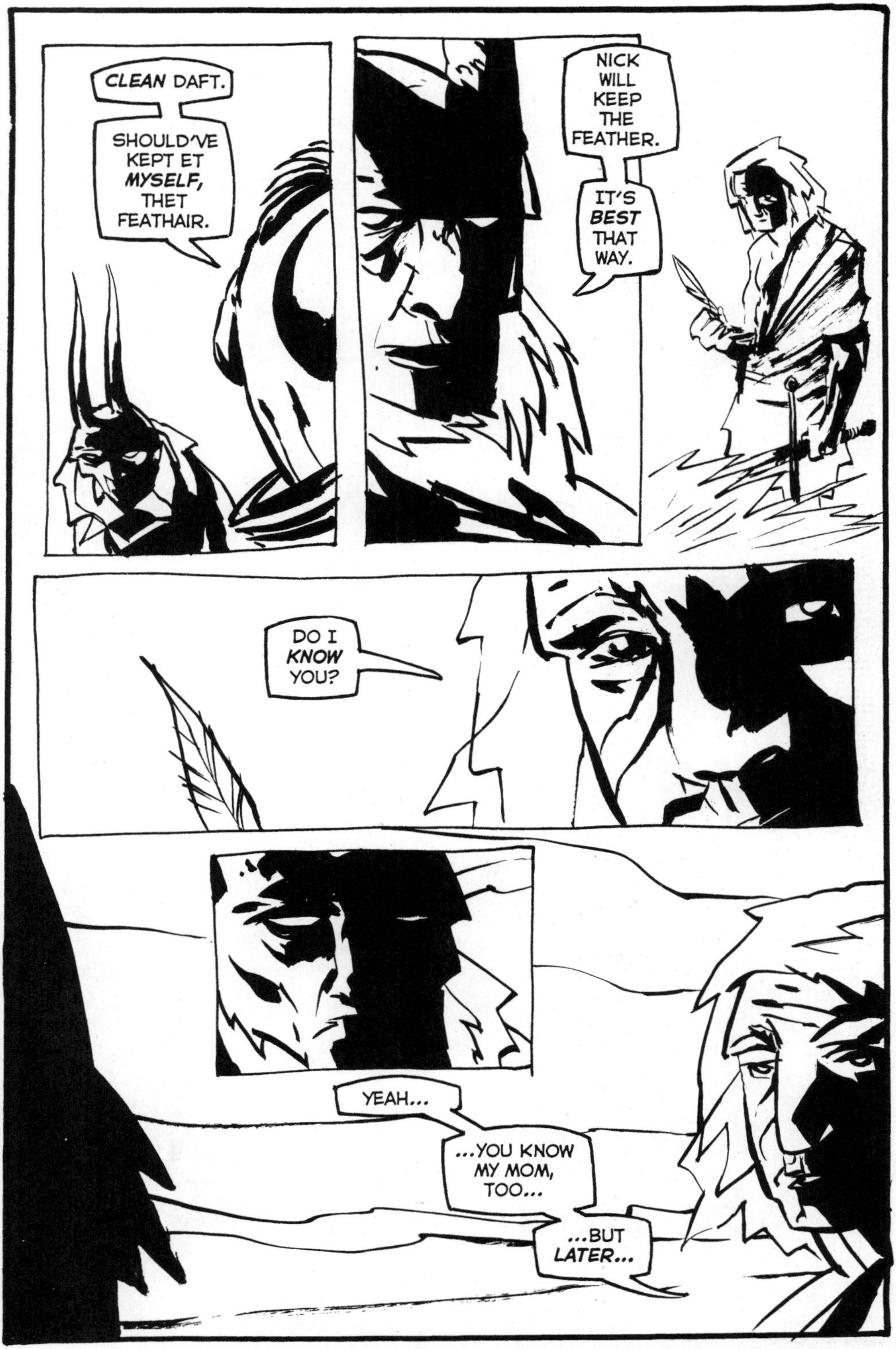
CLEAN DAFT.
SHOULD'VE KEPT ET MYSELF, THET FEATHAIR.
NICK WILL KEEP THE FEATHER.
IT'S BEST THAT WAY.
DO I KNOW YOU?
YEAH...
...YOU KNOW MY MOM, TOO...
...BUT LATER...

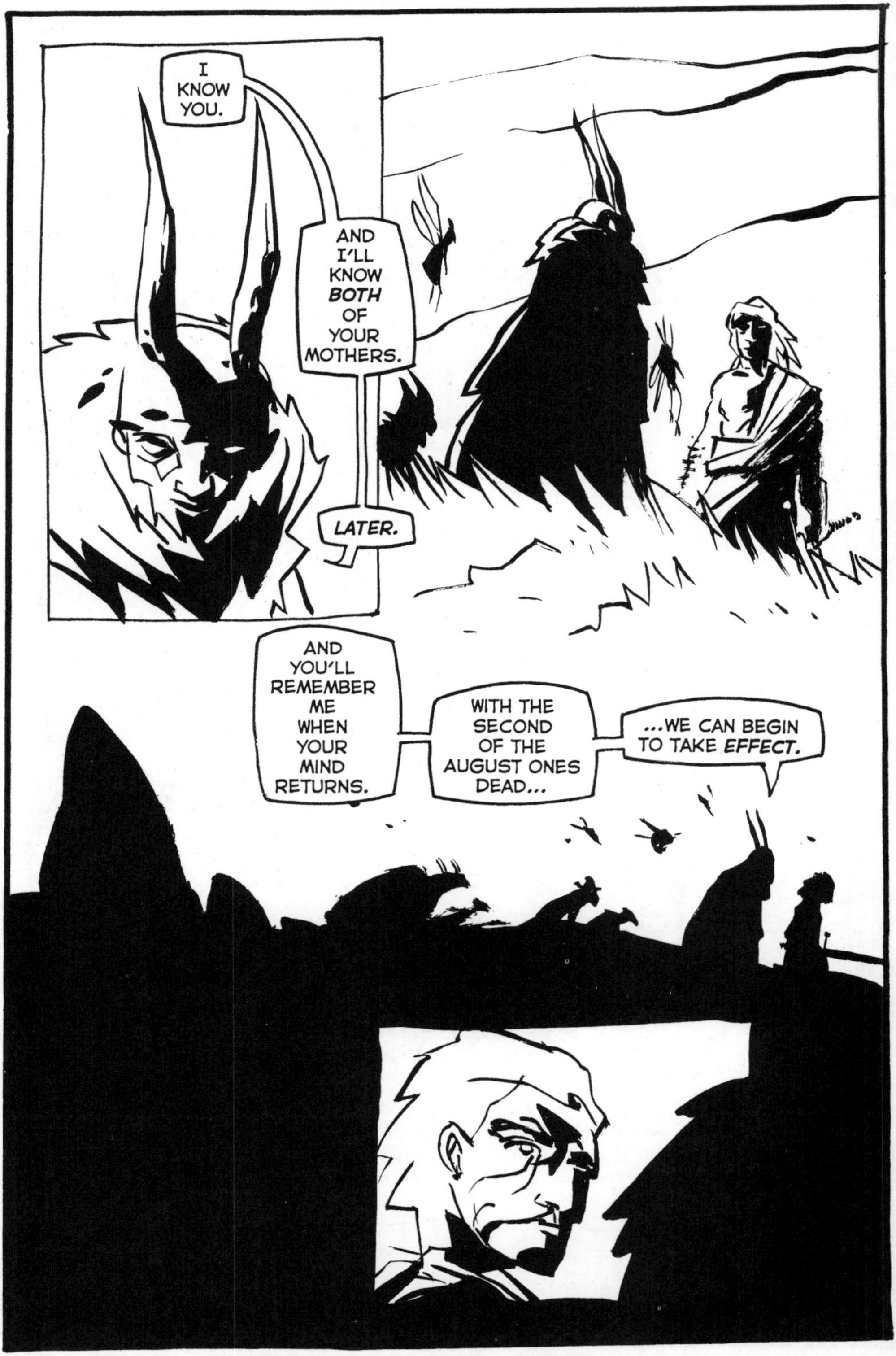
I KNOW YOU.
AND I'LL KNOW *BOTH* OF YOUR MOTHERS.
LATER.
AND YOU'LL REMEMBER ME WHEN YOUR MIND RETURNS.
WITH THE SECOND OF THE AUGUST ONES DEAD...
...WE CAN BEGIN TO TAKE *EFFECT.*

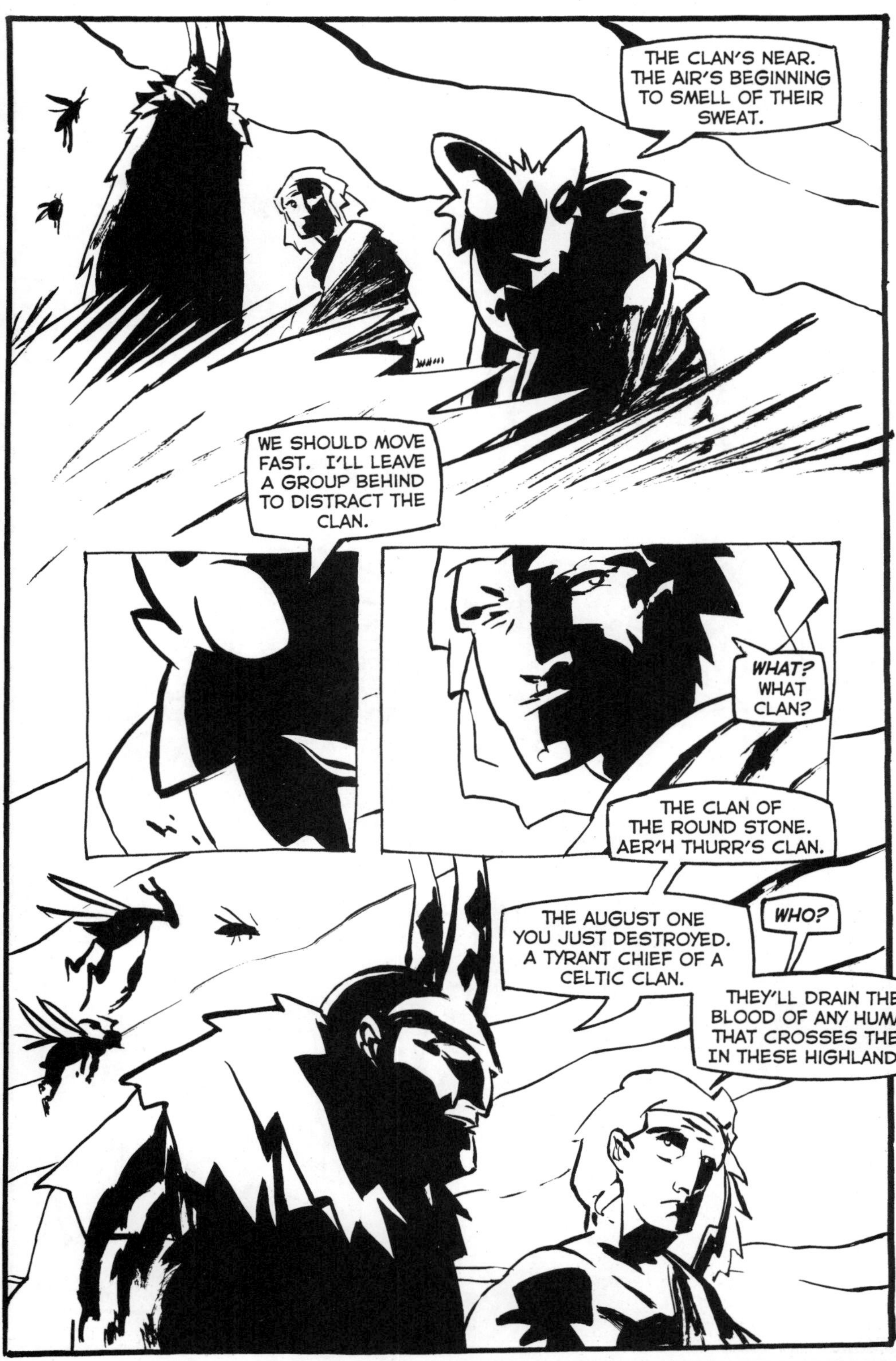
THE CLAN'S NEAR. THE AIR'S BEGINNING TO SMELL OF THEIR SWEAT.
WE SHOULD MOVE FAST. I'LL LEAVE A GROUP BEHIND TO DISTRACT THE CLAN.
WHAT? WHAT CLAN?
THE CLAN OF THE ROUND STONE. AER'H THURR'S CLAN.
WHO?
THE AUGUST ONE YOU JUST DESTROYED. A TYRANT CHIEF OF A CELTIC CLAN.
THEY'LL DRAIN THE BLOOD OF ANY HUMAN THAT CROSSES THEM IN THESE HIGHLANDS.

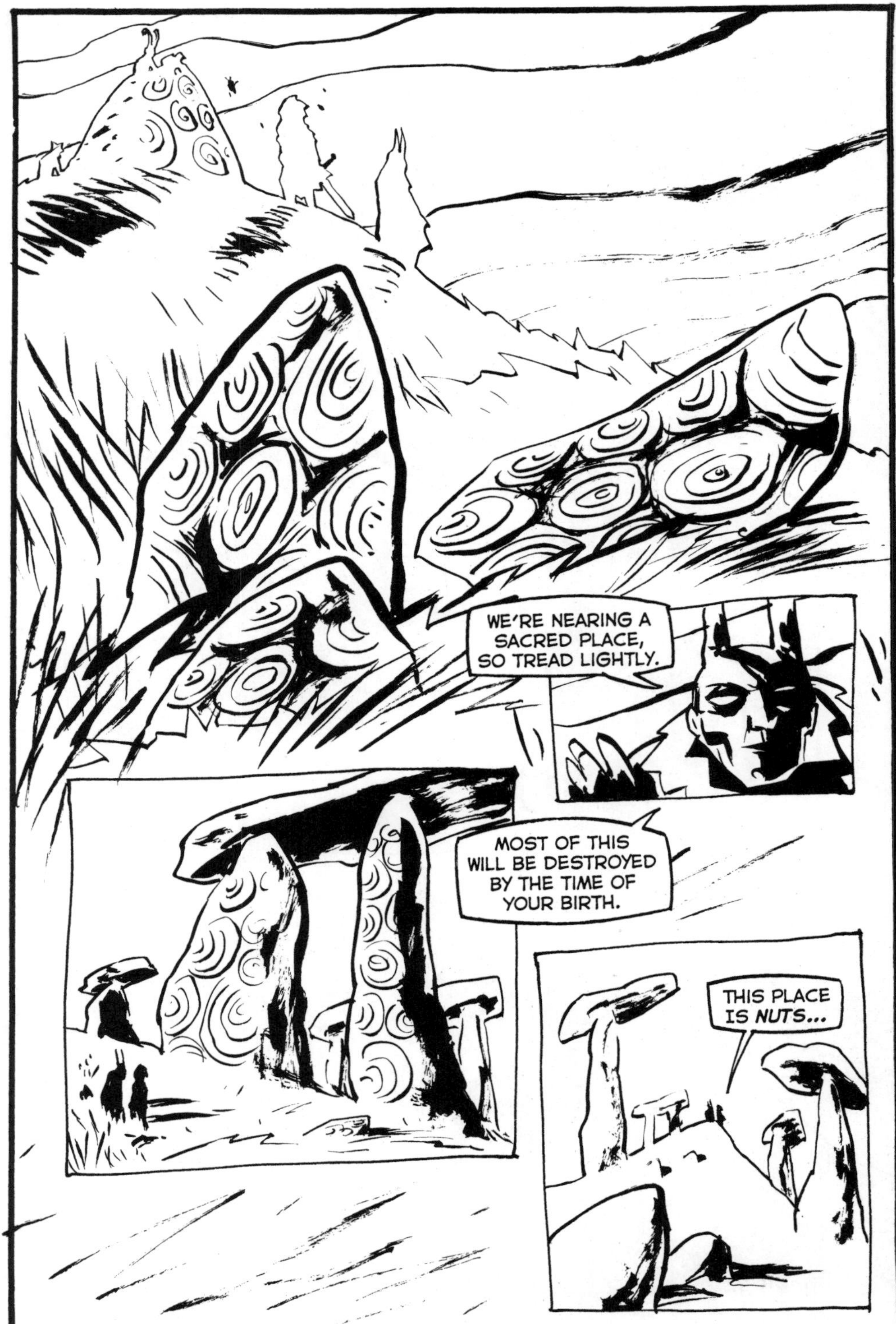
WE'RE NEARING A SACRED PLACE, SO TREAD LIGHTLY.
MOST OF THIS WILL BE DESTROYED BY THE TIME OF YOUR BIRTH.
THIS PLACE IS *NUTS...*

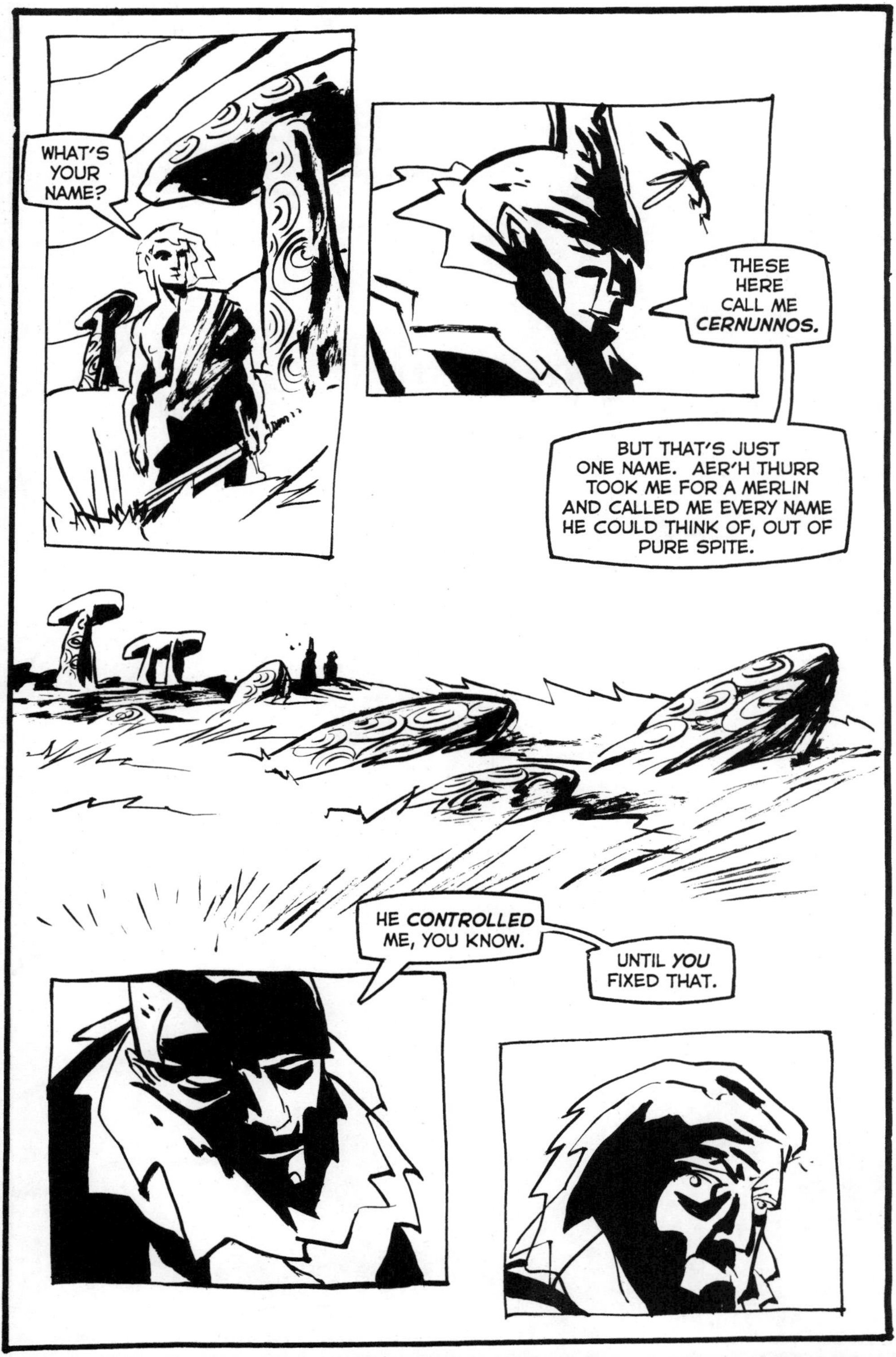
WHAT'S YOUR NAME?
THESE HERE CALL ME *CERNUNNOS.*
BUT THAT'S JUST ONE NAME. AER'H THURR TOOK ME FOR A MERLIN AND CALLED ME EVERY NAME HE COULD THINK OF, OUT OF PURE SPITE.
HE *CONTROLLED* ME, YOU KNOW.
UNTIL *YOU* FIXED THAT.

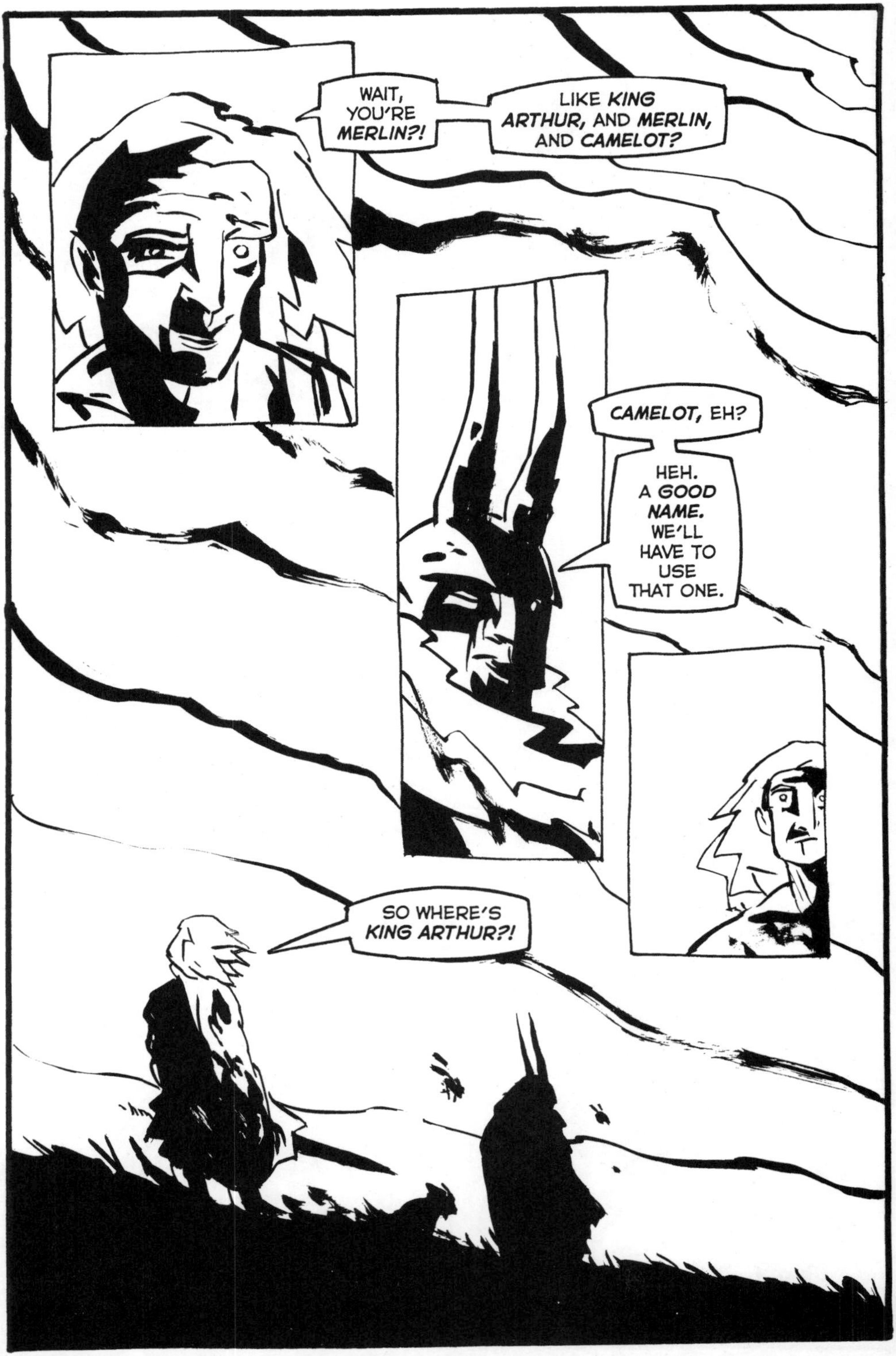
WAIT, YOU'RE MERLIN?!
LIKE KING ARTHUR, AND MERLIN, AND CAMELOT?
CAMELOT, EH?
HEH. A GOOD NAME. WE'LL HAVE TO USE THAT ONE.
SO WHERE'S KING ARTHUR?!

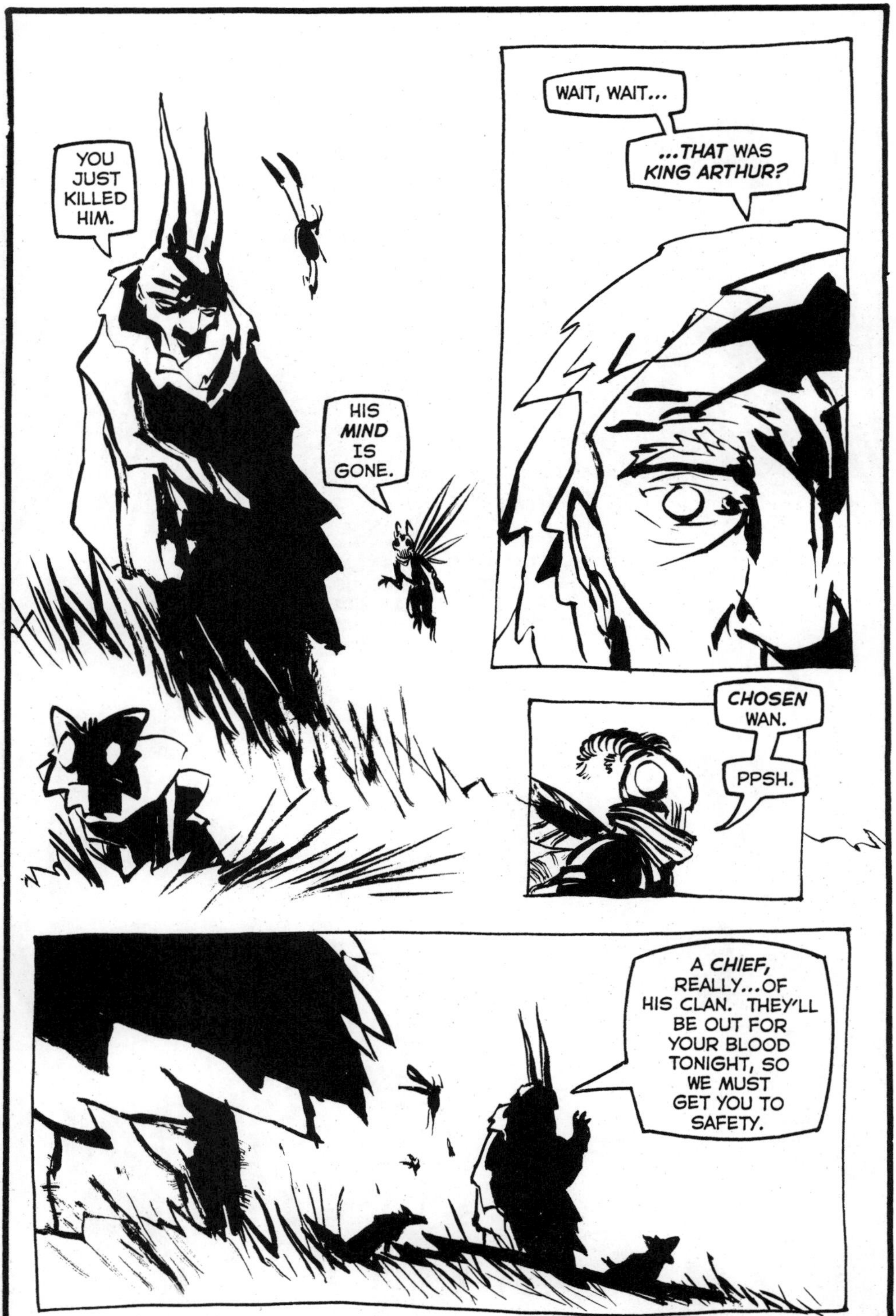
YOU JUST KILLED HIM.
HIS MIND IS GONE.
WAIT, WAIT...
...THAT WAS KING ARTHUR?
CHOSEN WAN.
PPSH.
A CHIEF, REALLY...OF HIS CLAN. THEY'LL BE OUT FOR YOUR BLOOD TONIGHT, SO WE MUST GET YOU TO SAFETY.

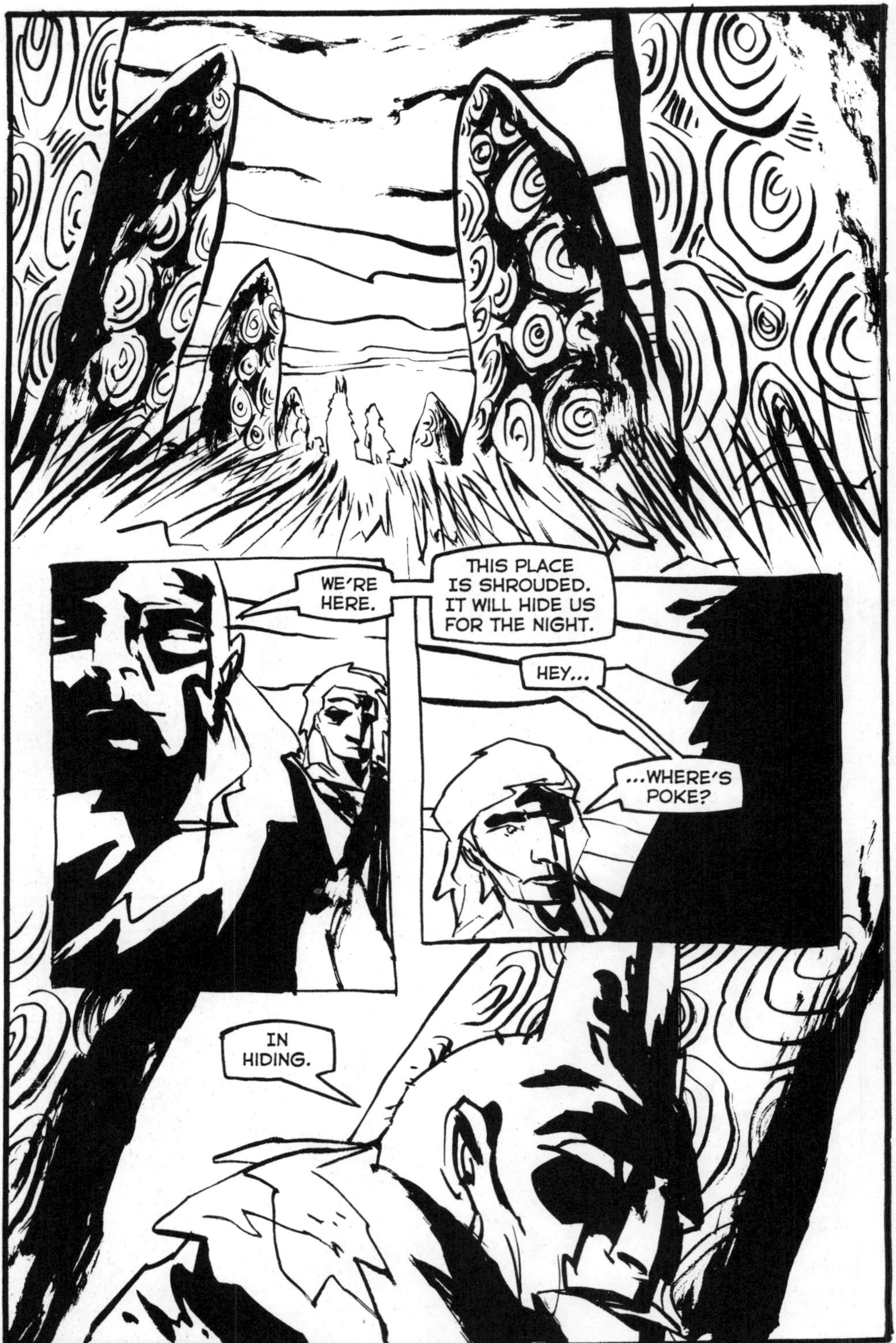
WE'RE HERE.
THIS PLACE IS SHROUDED. IT WILL HIDE US FOR THE NIGHT.
HEY...
...WHERE'S POKE?
IN HIDING.

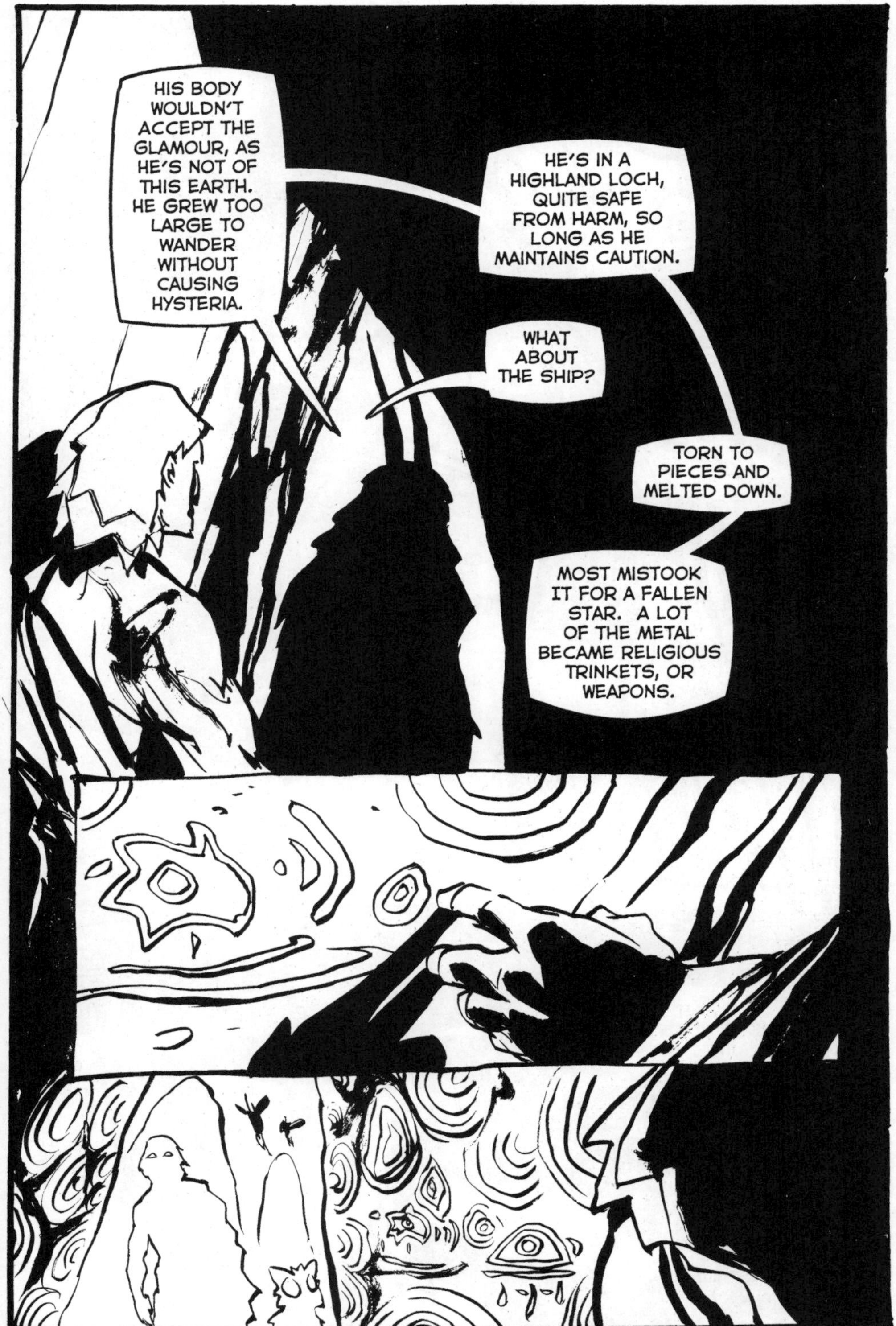
HIS BODY WOULDN'T ACCEPT THE GLAMOUR, AS HE'S NOT OF THIS EARTH. HE GREW TOO LARGE TO WANDER WITHOUT CAUSING HYSTERIA.
HE'S IN A HIGHLAND LOCH, QUITE SAFE FROM HARM, SO LONG AS HE MAINTAINS CAUTION.
WHAT ABOUT THE SHIP?
TORN TO PIECES AND MELTED DOWN.
MOST MISTOOK IT FOR A FALLEN STAR. A LOT OF THE METAL BECAME RELIGIOUS TRINKETS, OR WEAPONS.

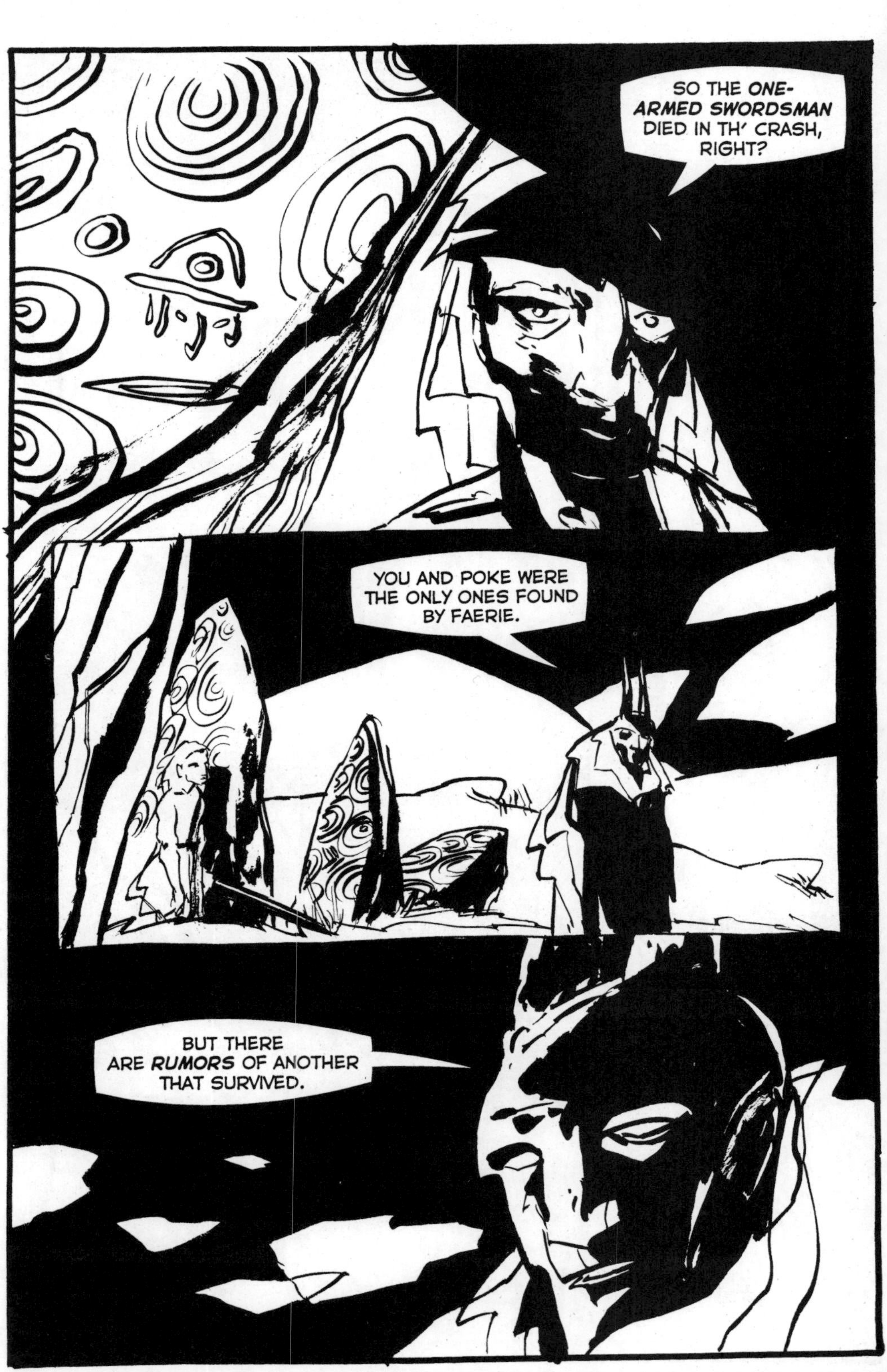
SO THE ONE-ARMED SWORDSMAN DIED IN TH' CRASH, RIGHT?
YOU AND POKE WERE THE ONLY ONES FOUND BY FAERIE.
BUT THERE ARE RUMORS OF ANOTHER THAT SURVIVED.

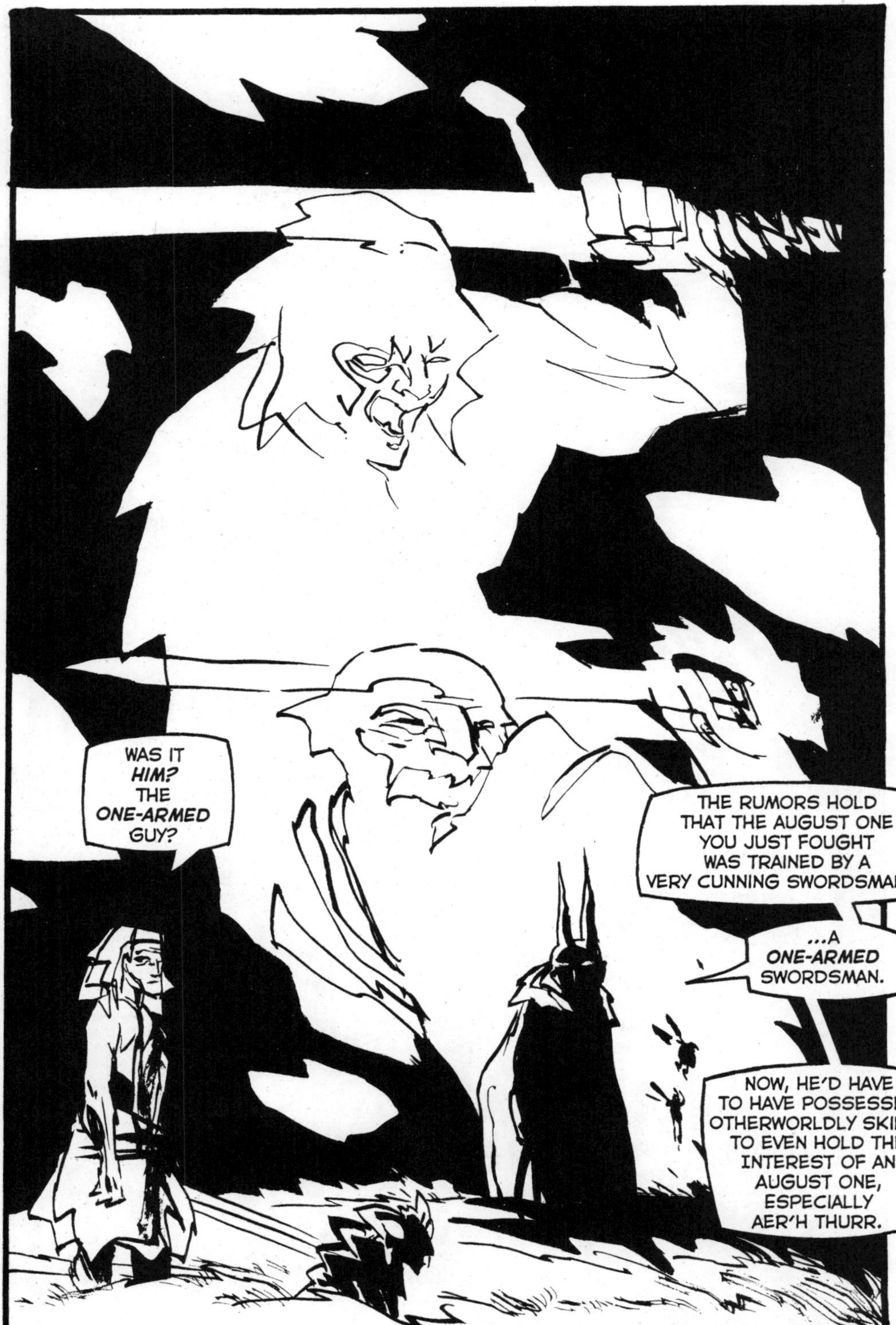
WAS IT *HIM?* THE *ONE-ARMED* GUY?
THE RUMORS HOLD THAT THE AUGUST ONE YOU JUST FOUGHT WAS TRAINED BY A VERY CUNNING SWORDSMAN..
...A *ONE-ARMED* SWORDSMAN.
NOW, HE'D HAVE TO HAVE POSSESSED OTHERWORLDLY SKILLS TO EVEN HOLD THE INTEREST OF AN AUGUST ONE, ESPECIALLY AER'H THURR.

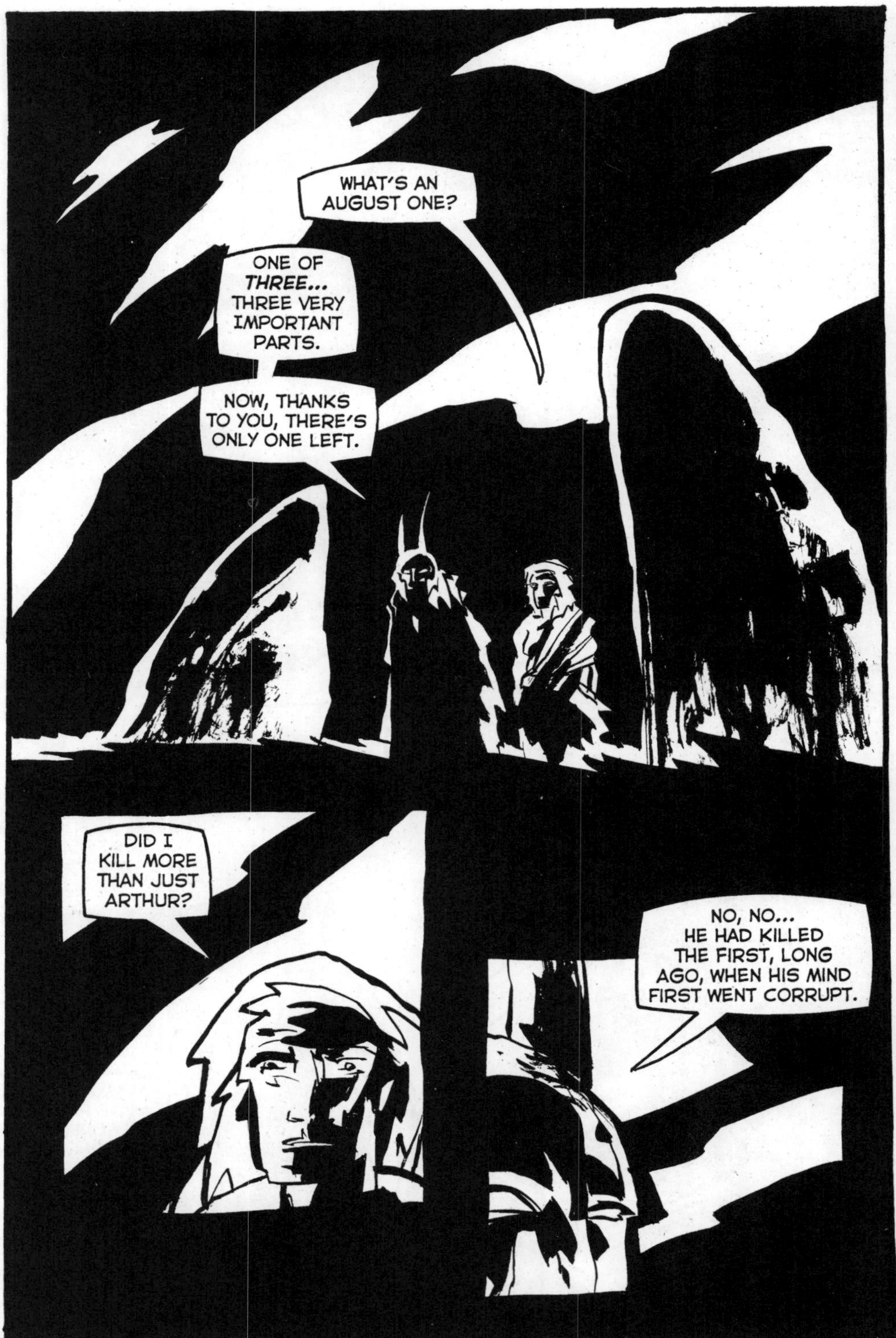
WHAT'S AN AUGUST ONE?
ONE OF *THREE...* THREE VERY IMPORTANT PARTS.
NOW, THANKS TO YOU, THERE'S ONLY ONE LEFT.
DID I KILL MORE THAN JUST ARTHUR?
NO, NO... HE HAD KILLED THE FIRST, LONG AGO, WHEN HIS MIND FIRST WENT CORRUPT.

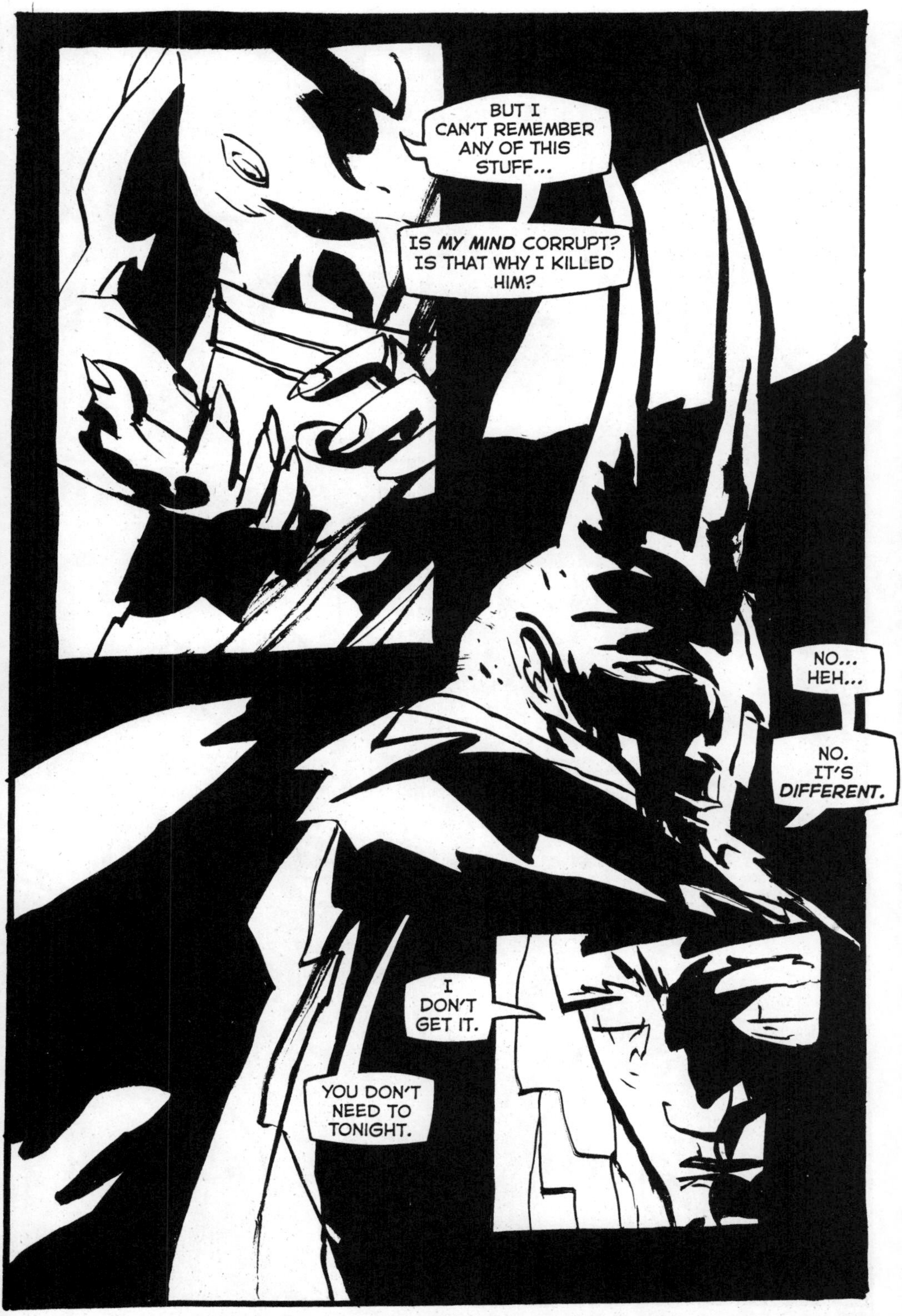
BUT I CAN'T REMEMBER ANY OF THIS STUFF...
IS *MY MIND* CORRUPT? IS THAT WHY I KILLED HIM?
NO... HEH...
NO. IT'S *DIFFERENT.*
I DON'T GET IT.
YOU DON'T NEED TO TONIGHT.

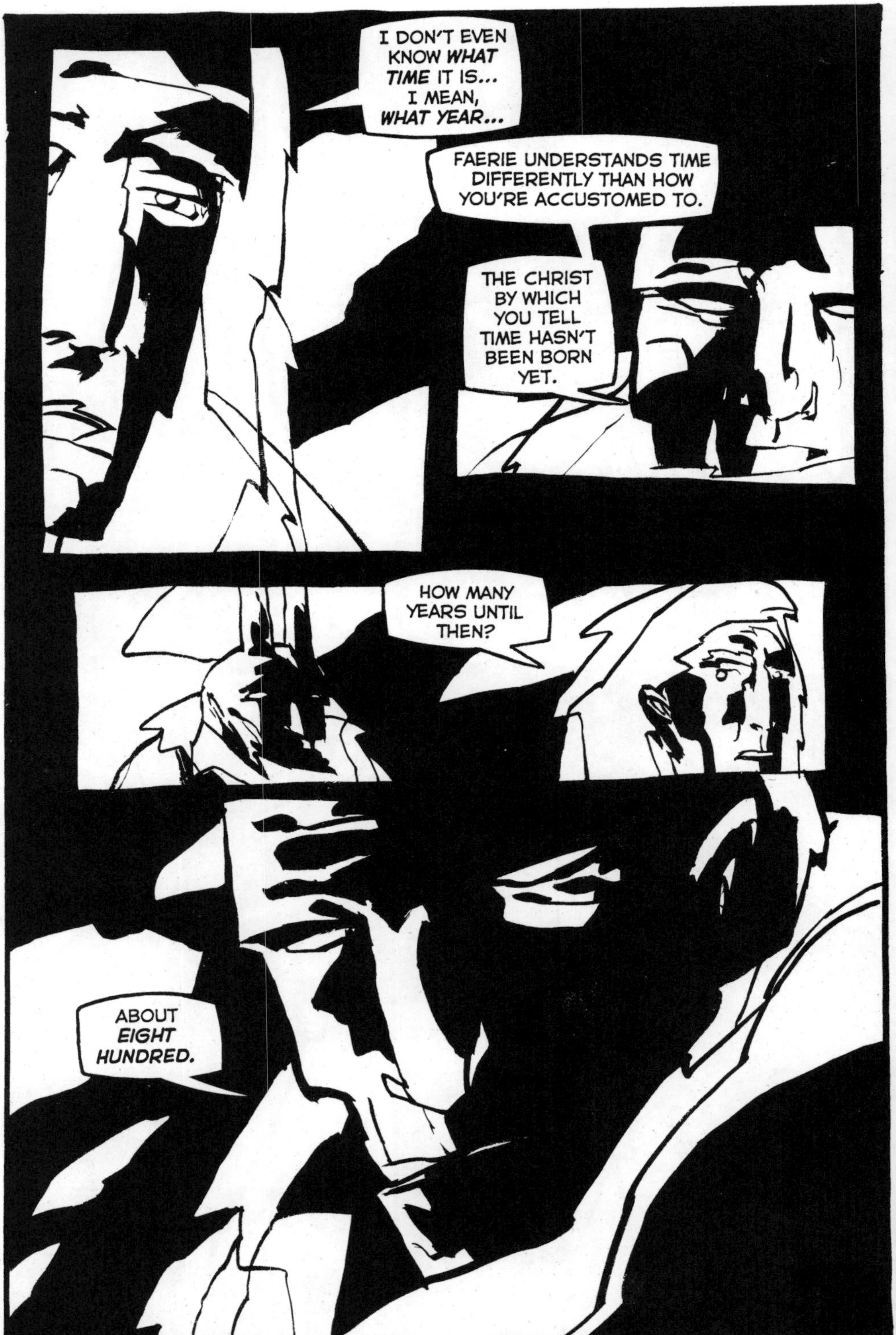
I DON'T EVEN KNOW *WHAT TIME* IT IS... I MEAN, *WHAT YEAR...*
FAERIE UNDERSTANDS TIME DIFFERENTLY THAN HOW YOU'RE ACCUSTOMED TO.
THE CHRIST BY WHICH YOU TELL TIME HASN'T BEEN BORN YET.
HOW MANY YEARS UNTIL THEN?
ABOUT *EIGHT HUNDRED.*

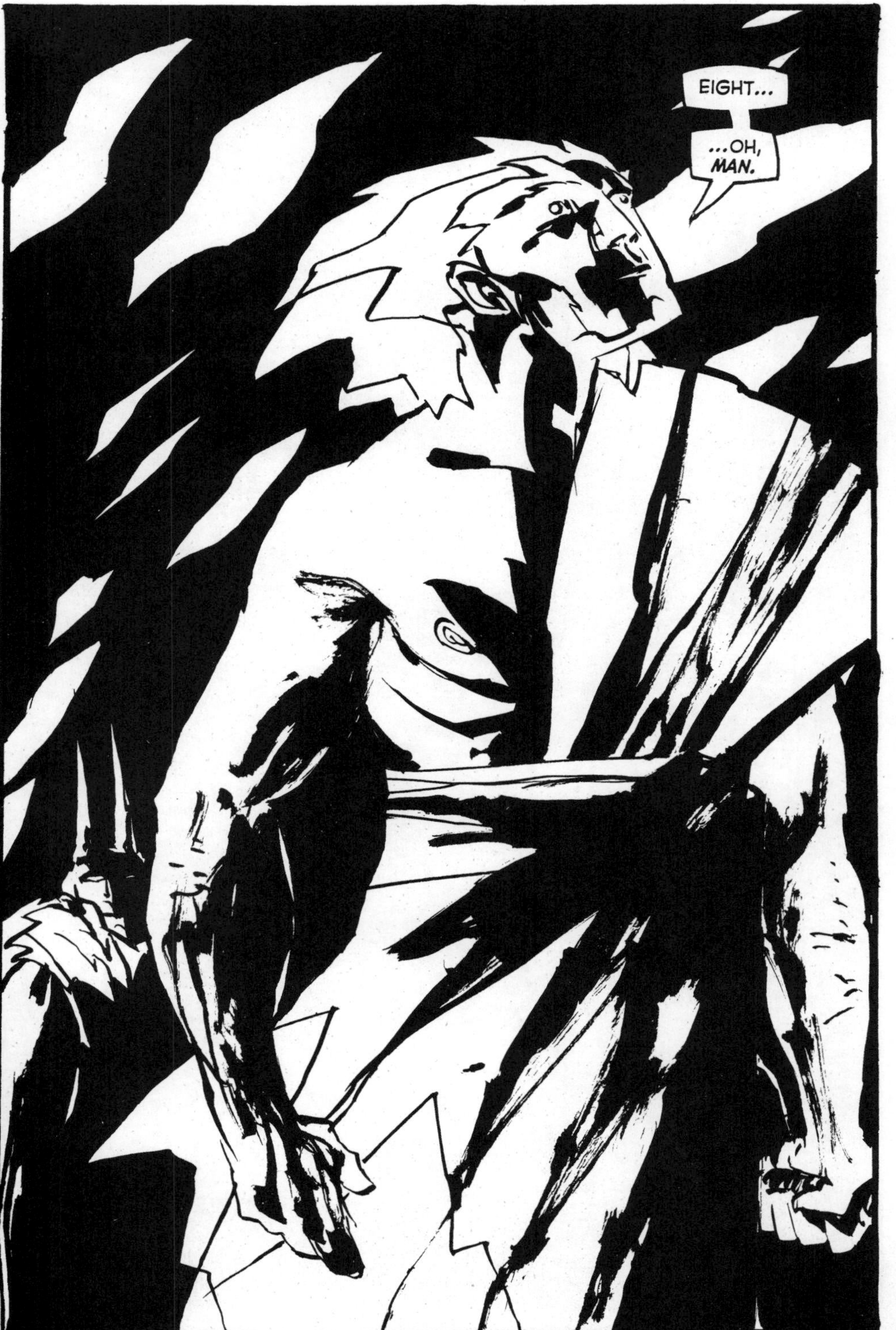
EIGHT...
...OH, *MAN.*

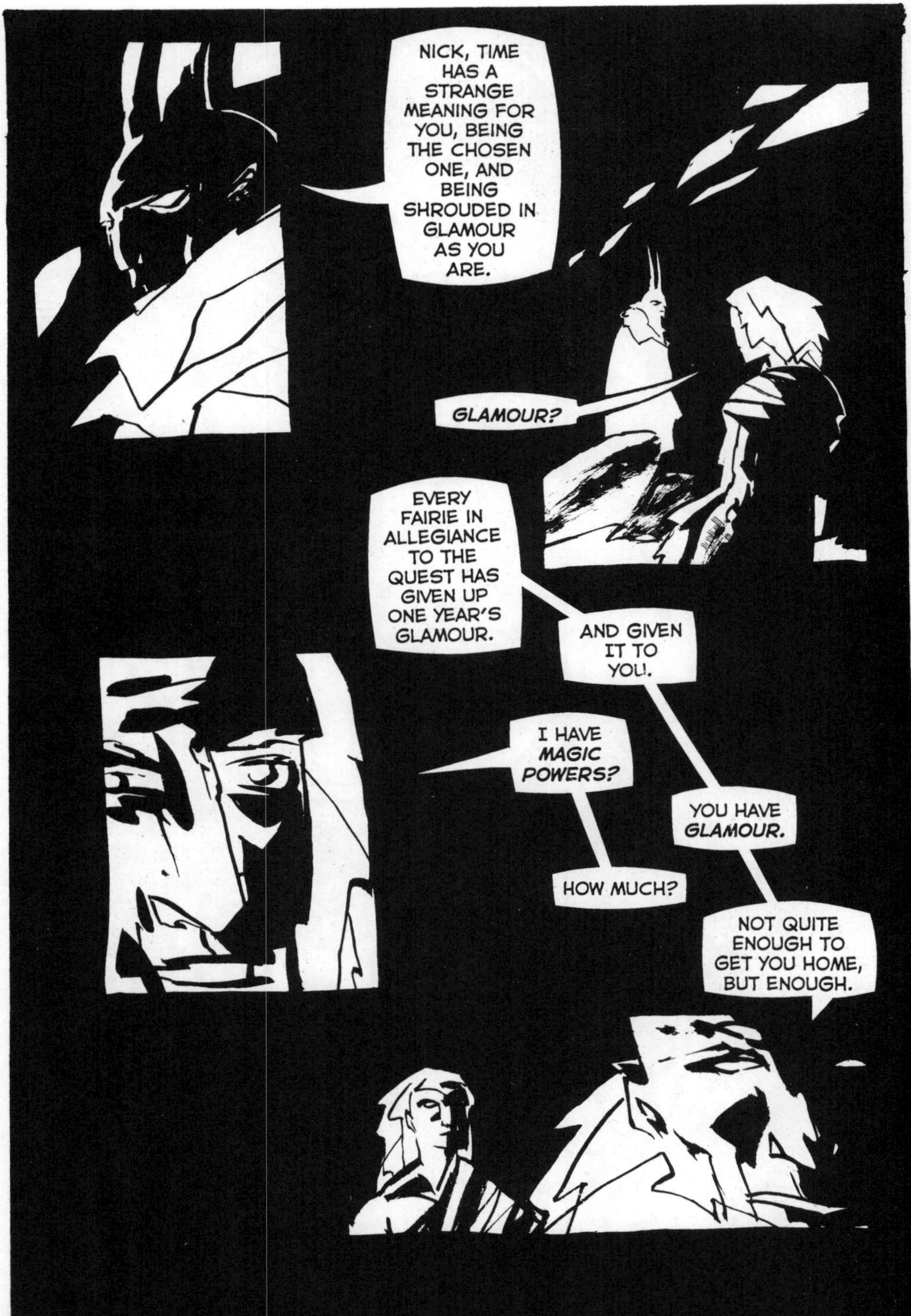
NICK, TIME HAS A STRANGE MEANING FOR YOU, BEING THE CHOSEN ONE, AND BEING SHROUDED IN GLAMOUR AS YOU ARE.
GLAMOUR?
EVERY FAIRIE IN ALLEGIANCE TO THE QUEST HAS GIVEN UP ONE YEAR'S GLAMOUR.
AND GIVEN IT TO YOU.
I HAVE *MAGIC POWERS?*
YOU HAVE *GLAMOUR.*
HOW MUCH?
NOT QUITE ENOUGH TO GET YOU HOME, BUT ENOUGH.

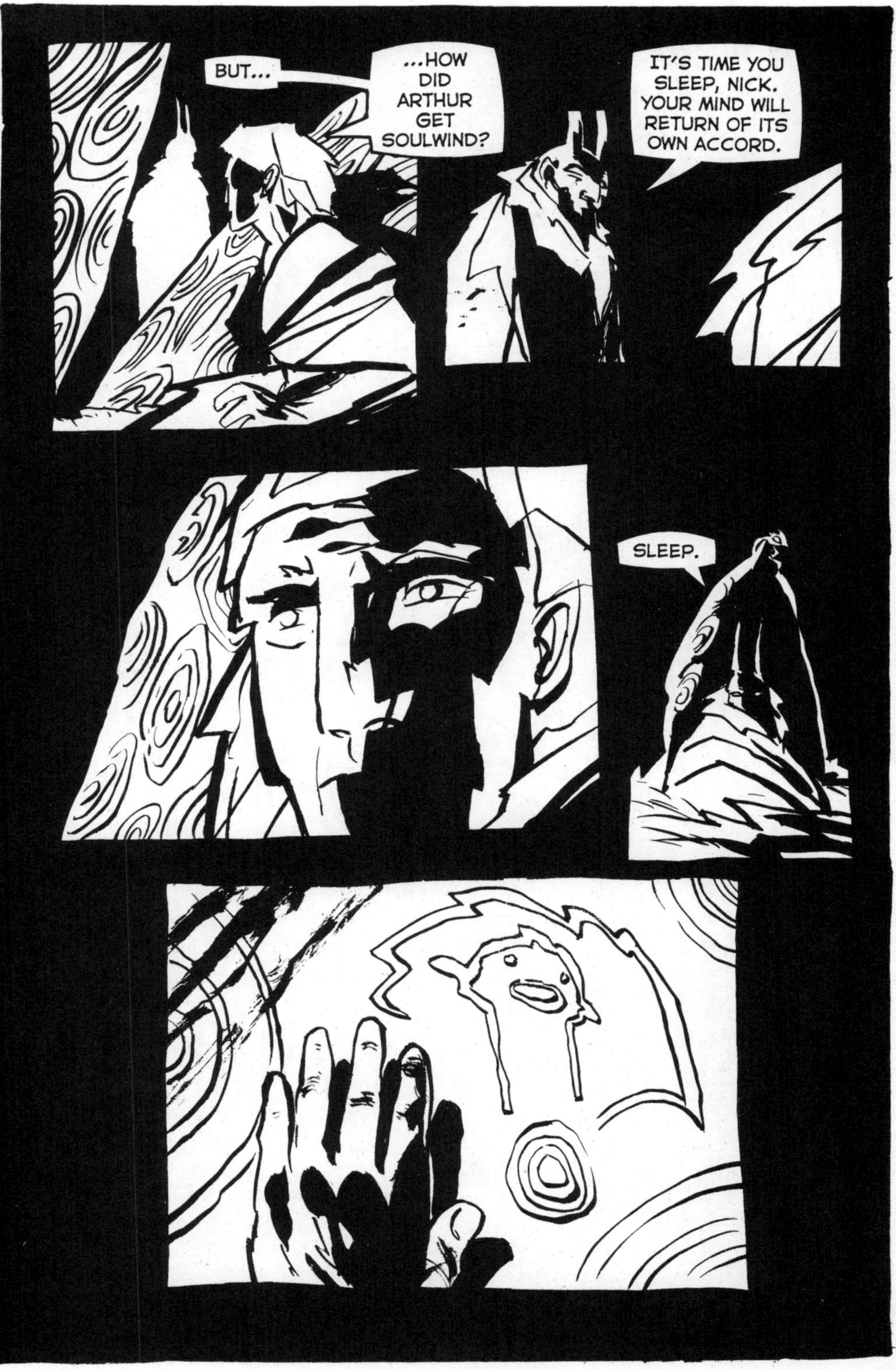
BUT...
...HOW DID ARTHUR GET SOULWIND?
IT'S TIME YOU SLEEP, NICK. YOUR MIND WILL RETURN OF ITS OWN ACCORD.
SLEEP.

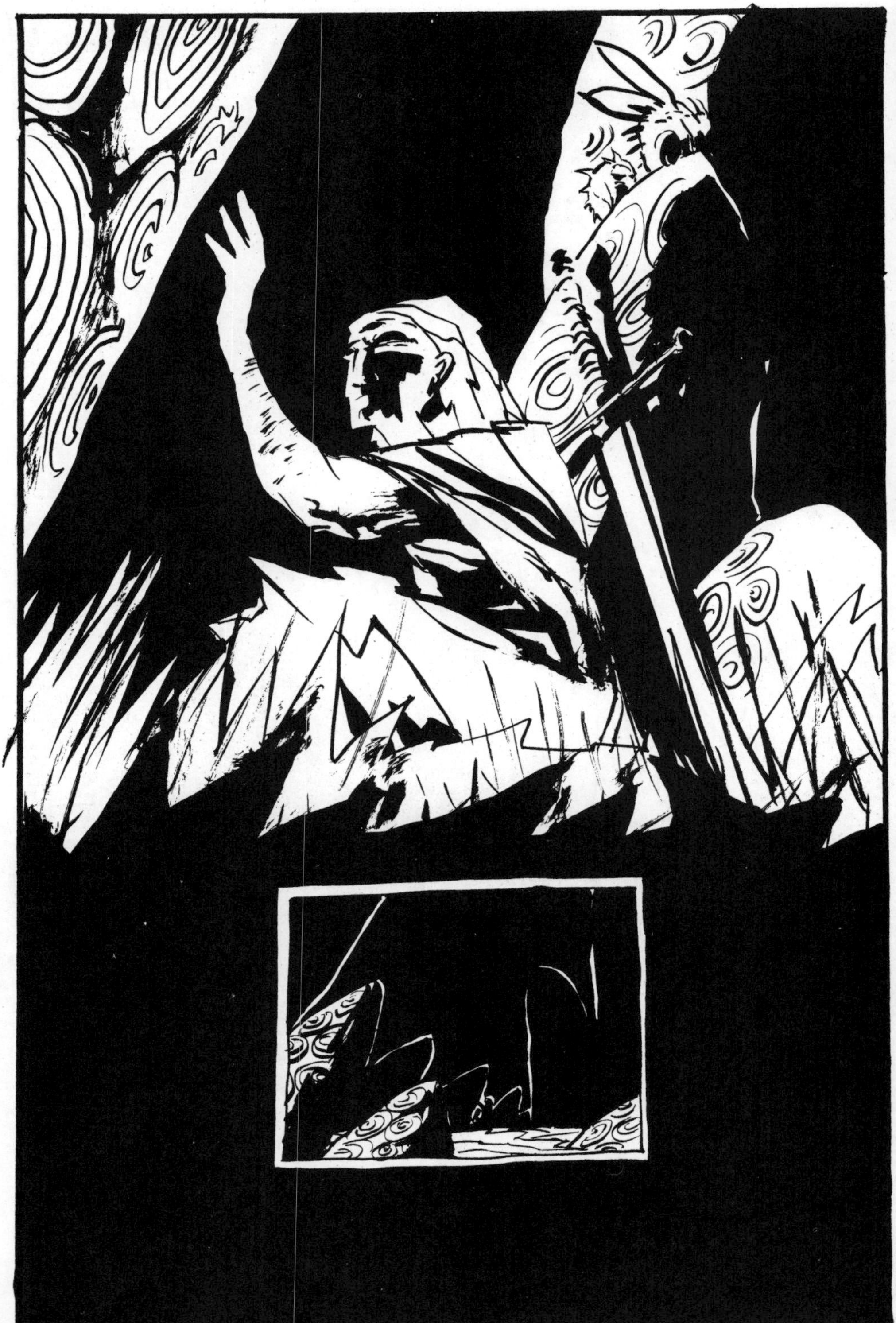

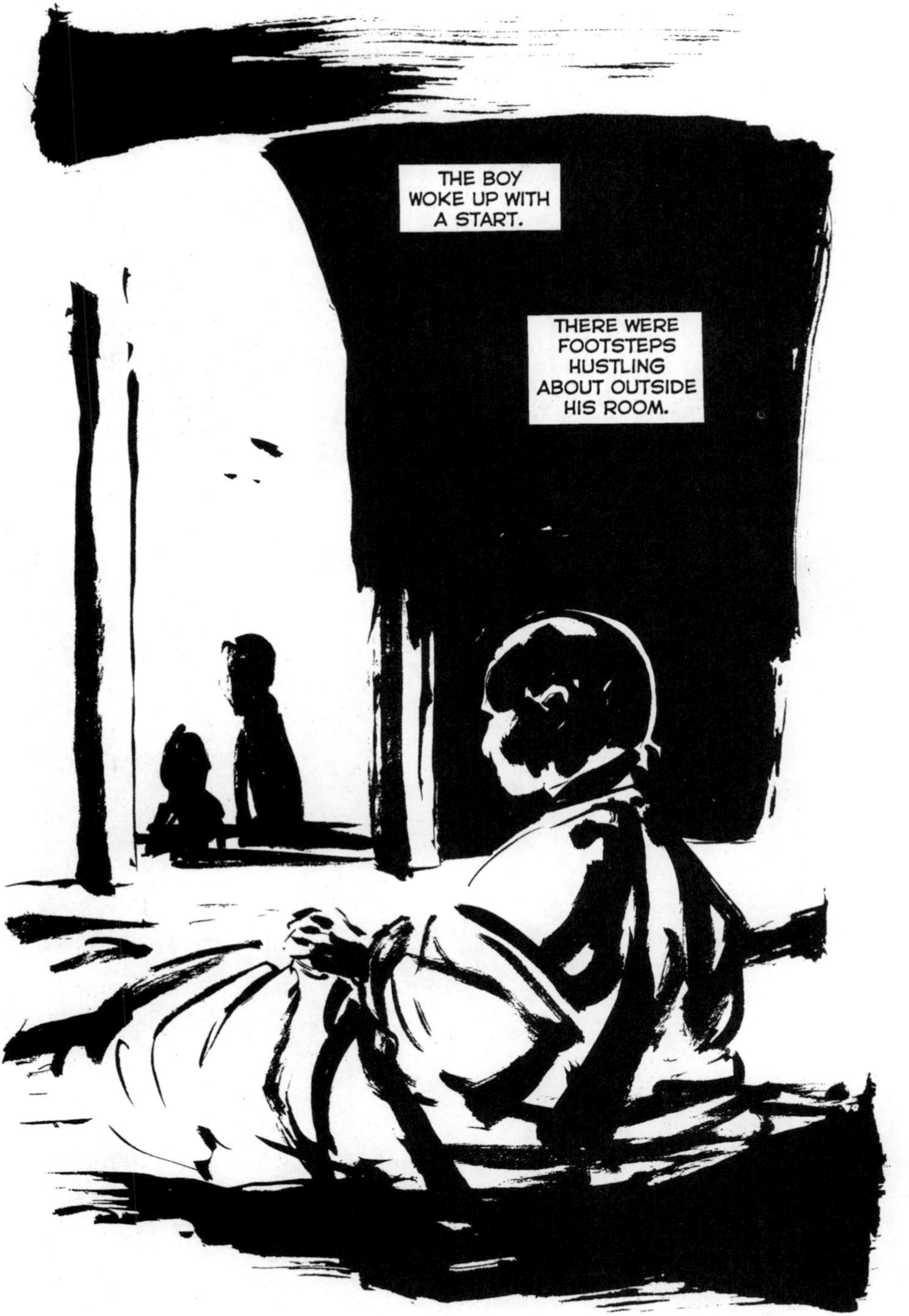
THE BOY WOKE UP WITH A START.
THERE WERE FOOTSTEPS HUSTLING ABOUT OUTSIDE HIS ROOM.

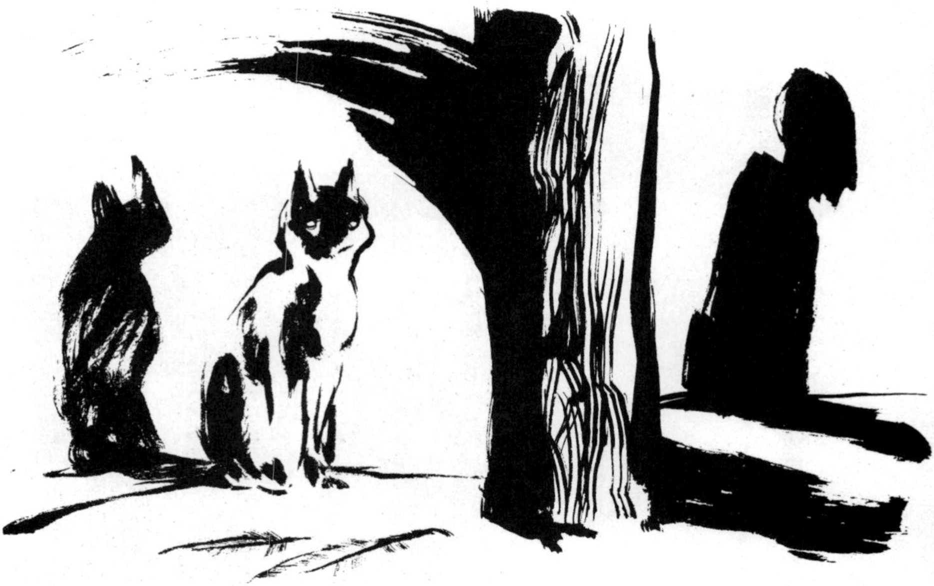

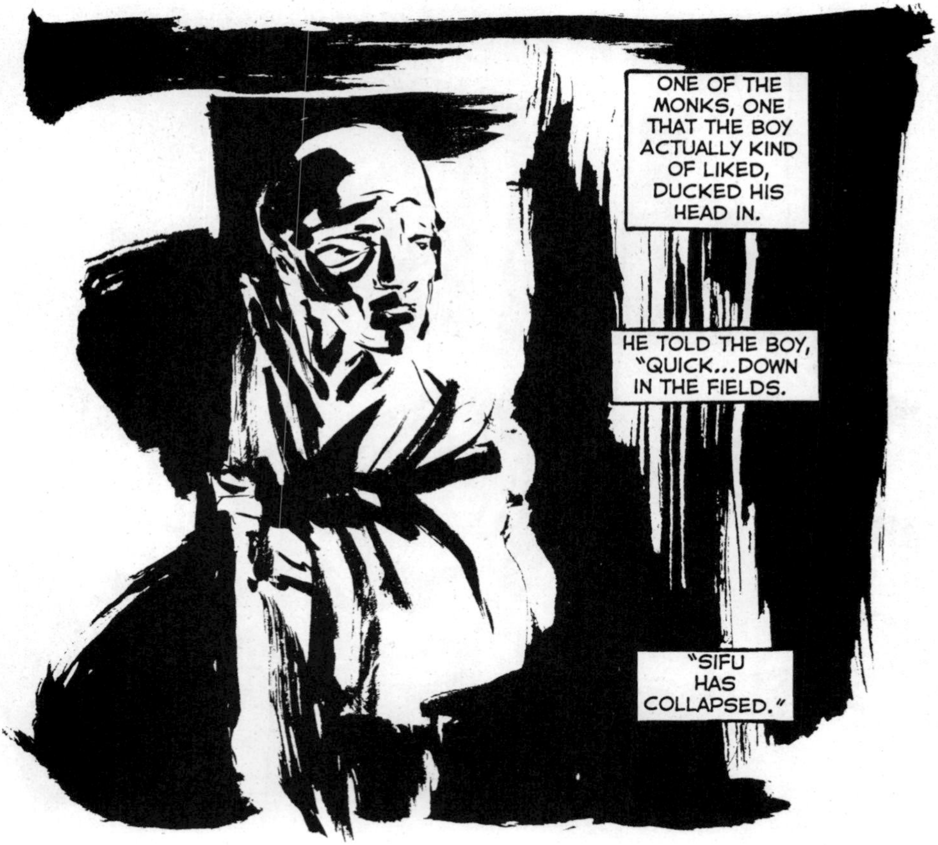
ONE OF THE MONKS, ONE THAT THE BOY ACTUALLY KIND OF LIKED, DUCKED HIS HEAD IN.
HE TOLD THE BOY, "QUICK...DOWN IN THE FIELDS.
"SIFU HAS COLLAPSED."

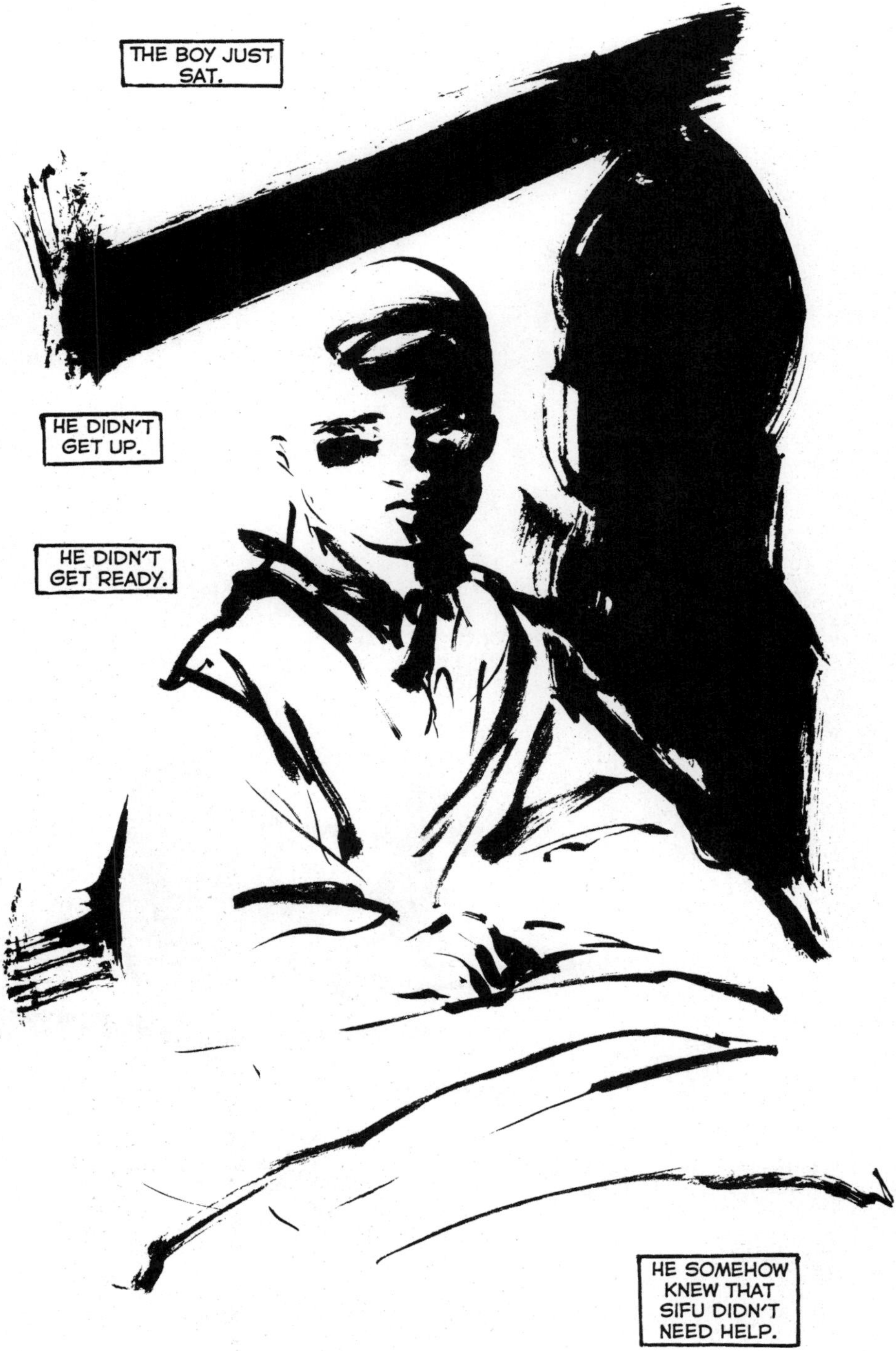
THE BOY JUST SAT.
HE DIDN'T GET UP.
HE DIDN'T GET READY.
HE SOMEHOW KNEW THAT SIFU DIDN'T NEED HELP.